Money, Inflation and the Constitutional Position of the Central Bank

Money, Inflation and the Constitutional Position of the Central Bank

MILTON FRIEDMAN
CHARLES A. E. GOODHART

With an extended introduction by Geoffrey E. Wood

Including the
THIRTY-SECOND WINCOTT LECTURE
8 OCTOBER 2002

The Institute of Economic Affairs

First published in Great Britain in 2003 by
The Institute of Economic Affairs
2 Lord North Street
Westminster
London sw1p 3lb
in association with Profile Books Ltd

The mission of the Institute of Economic Affairs is to improve public understanding of the fundamental institutions of a free society, with particular reference to the role of markets in solving economic and social problems.

A CIP catalogue record for this book is available from the British Library.

ISBN 0 255 36538 1

Many IEA publications are translated into languages other than English or are reprinted. Permission to translate or to reprint should be sought from the General Director at the address above.

Typeset in Stone by MacGuru Ltd
info@macguru.org.uk

Printed and bound in Great Britain by Hobbs the Printers

CONTENTS

THE AUTHORS

Geoffrey E. Wood

Geoffrey Wood is Professor of Economics at the Sir John Cass Business School, City of London. He has also taught at the University of Warwick, and been on the research staff of the Bank of England and the Federal Reserve Bank of St Louis. He has published extensively in the areas of monetary economics and international economics. Among these publications are, for the IEA, *Too Much Money?*, with Gordon Pepper (Hobart Paper 68, 1975); *Independence for the Bank of England?*, with Forrest Capie and Terry Mills (Current Controversies 4, 1993); *The Right Road to Monetary Union Revisited*, with John Chown and Max Beber (Current Controversies 8, 1994); *Fifty Economic Fallacies Exposed* (Occasional Paper 129, 2002). He is a member of the IEA's Academic Advisory Council and a trustee of the Wincott Foundation.

Milton Friedman

Milton Friedman was born in 1912 in New York City and graduated from Rutgers before taking an MA at Chicago and a PhD at Columbia. In 1935–37 he worked for the US National Resources Committee, in 1937–40 for the National Bureau of Economic

Research, and in 1941–43 for the US Treasury. From 1946 to 1977 he taught at the University of Chicago.

Milton Friedman is now a Senior Research Fellow at the Hoover Institution of Stanford University, California, and Paul Snowden Russell Distinguished Service Professor Emeritus of Economics at the University of Chicago. He has taught at universities throughout the world, from Cambridge to Tokyo. Since 1946 he has also been on the research staff of the National Bureau of Economic Research.

He is known to a wider audience as an advocate of a volunteer army (in place of the US draft), reverse income tax (in place of partial or universalist poverty programmes), monetary policy and floating exchange rates. He is the acknowledged head of the 'Chicago School' which specialises in the empirical testing of policy propositions derived from market analysis. Professor Friedman was awarded the 1976 Nobel Prize in Economic Sciences.

Among his best-known books are *Essays in Positive Economics* (Chicago, 1953), *Studies in the Quantity Theory of Money* (edited by Friedman, Chicago, 1956), A *Theory of the Consumption Function* (Princeton, 1957), *Capitalism and Freedom* (Chicago, 1962), (with Anna J. Schwartz) *A Monetary History of the United States, 1867–1960* (Princeton, 1963), and *The Optimum Quantity of Money* (Aldine, Chicago, and Macmillan, London, 1969). The IEA has published his *Monetary Correction* (Occasional Paper 41, 1974), *From Galbraith to Economic Freedom* (Occasional Paper 49, 1977), *Inflation and Unemployment: The New Dimension of Politics* (the 1976 Alfred Nobel Memorial Lecture, Occasional Paper 51, 1977), and his contributions to *Inflation: Causes, Consequences, Cures* (IEA Readings No. 14, 1974).

Milton Friedman was awarded the Presidential Medal of

Freedom in 1988 and received the National Medal of Science the same year. He is a past President of the American Economic Association.

On 9 May 2002 the Cato Institute, Washington DC, inaugurated the Milton Friedman Prize for Advancing Liberty. The first recipient (posthumously) was Lord Peter Bauer – see *A Tribute to Peter Bauer* (IEA Occasional Paper 128, 2002).

Charles A. E. Goodhart

Charles Goodhart is a graduate of Cambridge and Harvard. He has held academic positions at the University of Cambridge and at the London School of Economics. He has also worked as a monetary economist at the Bank of England, and more recently as Special Adviser to the Governor of the Bank of England. He was elected a Fellow of the British Academy in 1990, and awarded the CBE in the New Year's Honours List for 1997, for services to monetary economics. During 1986, he helped to found, with Professor Mervyn King, the Financial Markets Group at LSE. He served as an independent member of the Monetary Policy Committee from 1997 to 2000.

Goodhart's publications include *The New York Money Market, 1900–1913*; *The Business of Banking, 1891–1914*; and *Money, Information and Uncertainty*, which has been revised. On financial regulation, he has also authored, edited or co-authored: *Financial Regulation: Why, how and where now?*; *Which Lender of Last Resort for Europe?*; *Regulating Financial Services and Markets in the 21st Century*; and *Financial Crises, Contagion, and the Lender of Last Resort*.

He is, perhaps, more widely known for two less serious pieces.

He was one of the first people to undertake a serious empirical study of the relationship between macroeconomic developments and political popularity, in his article 'Political Economy' (*Political Studies*, vol. 18, 1970). Second, he is the author of Goodhart's Law: 'that any observed statistical regularity will tend to collapse once pressure is placed upon it for control purposes'.

In his free time he is a sheep farmer, an exercise that uses up any spare cash he may have earned elsewhere.

FOREWORD

This collection of readings brings together three contributions to economic thought. The IEA is pleased to publish the 2002 Wincott lecture, delivered by Professor Charles Goodhart, entitled 'The Constitutional Position of the Central Bank'. This is an important contribution to the analysis of how a central bank should be structured within a country's political system. In addition, to provide a broader context for the conduct of monetary policy, the IEA is taking this opportunity to republish two seminal works by Professor Milton Friedman, *The Counter-Revolution in Monetary Theory* (which was the first Wincott lecture) and *Unemployment versus Inflation? An Evaluation of the Phillips Curve*, previously published by the IEA as Occasional Papers 33 and 44 in 1970 and 1975 respectively. The three papers, together with the introduction by Professor Geoffrey Wood, provide an excellent review of the causes and consequences of inflation and of the way in which the procedures for the conduct of monetary policy can be embedded in a country's constitution to achieve the objective of a stable price level.

A reasonably stable price level is one of several necessary conditions for a stable and prosperous economy. There are, in turn, several necessary conditions for a stable price level, none of which was met in the period 1945–76. The first of these conditions is that policy-makers accept that there is no long-run benefit, in terms of higher output or employment, from higher inflation. The second is that policy-makers understand the cause of inflation: excess monetary growth. The third is that we have the correct institutional structure to ensure that intermediate target variables, such as monetary growth, are effectively controlled to achieve the end objective of a stable price level.

Readings 57 considers all these issues to paint a complete picture of the cause of inflation, the consequences of inflation and a mechanism for achieving low inflation. One of the essays by Professor Friedman, 'The Counter-Revolution in Monetary Theory', is a classical exposition of the argument for controlling monetary growth in order to control inflation. The other, 'Unemployment versus Inflation?', not only explains why there is no long-run trade-off between inflation and unemployment but also explains the evidence of the Phillips curve, showing an *apparent* trade-off between inflation and unemployment, in terms of the theory developed within the essay. This essay has become required reading for many undergraduate economics courses and should remain so as part of this new volume.

Both of the Friedman texts anticipate the development of important elements of economic theory over the following 25 years. Issues such as the crowding out of other economic activity by fiscal expansion, the transmission mechanism of monetary policy through asset prices and the crucial role that 'expectations' play in governing economic behaviour are all introduced in the Friedman essays and occupy the research time of many economists today.

It appears that an increased understanding of the causes and consequences of inflation in the late 1970s and 1980s did not automatically lead to the development of a stable price level. Policy-makers from 1976 onwards tried money supply targeting, exchange-rate targeting, fixed exchange-rate regimes and other mechanisms to try to reduce inflation. Some of these methods were temporarily successful and others failed. However, it is clear that the correct institutional structure that would enable the government to sustain the right policies to maintain a stable price level was not immediately discovered.

Professor Goodhart, an adviser to the Governor of the Bank of England, writes in his 2002 Wincott Memorial Lecture of the success of independent central banks in delivering the goal of low inflation that politicians acting with the best of intentions had failed to deliver. There is no 'democractic deficit' when making central banks independent of day-to-day control by politicians because the objectives of the central bank are still determined by the government. If an occasion arose whereby the short-term trade-off between output and inflation became important, there is a mechanism by which the government can express a view to the central bank. But, importantly, it must do so explicitly. An independent central bank lends 'credibility' to monetary policy. Markets believe that inflation targets will be met. Expectations are influenced and the short-term costs of reducing inflation are lower as a result. Goodhart also comments on the importance of not giving a central bank multiple objectives. Such objectives might conflict with each other and would raise issues that should be addressed in the political domain.

The essay by Geoffrey Wood links the Goodhart and Friedman essays and puts the Friedman essays in their historical context. In doing so, Wood raises a very important issue. The fact that central banks do not always directly target money supply aggregates or directly control them, instead preferring to use intermediate instruments such as short-term interest rates, does not mean that excess monetary growth is not the cause of inflation. It is. Many commentators today stress that 'increased competition' or 'lack of cost pressure' are responsible for today's benign inflation environment. They are not. If we do not wish to relive the experience of the 1970s we must continually remind ourselves of the causes and consequences of inflation and always seek better institutional mechanisms for delivering a stable price level. Such issues are fundamental to any basic training in economics, and this volume is a fine exposition of these issues.

The views expressed in Readings 57 are, as in all IEA publications, those of the author and not those of the Institute (which has no corporate view), its managing trustees, Academic Advisory Council members or senior staff.

PHILIP BOOTH

Editorial and Programme Director
Institute of Economic Affairs
Professor of Insurance and Risk Management
Sir John Cass Business School, City University
April 2003

ACKNOWLEDGEMENTS

I am most grateful to the Wincott Trustees for honouring me with the invitation to present the 2002 Wincott lecture. I would especially like to thank the Chairman of the Trustees, Sir Geoffrey Owen, for his great kindness and help in organising the occasion.

I am grateful to all my friends and colleagues at the Financial Markets Group at the London School of Economics, and at the Bank of England, particularly my companions on the Monetary Policy Committee, for their support, advice and assistance over many years. But all the views, and errors, remain my own. I would also like to thank my secretary, Marina Emond, for her assistance in the preparation of this paper, for which I am extremely grateful.

CHARLES A. E. GOODHART

SUMMARY

- Except in the short term, unemployment cannot be reduced by creating inflation.
- Even in the short term, unemployment can only be decreased by creating inflation if people are 'surprised' by the increase in the price level.
- As soon as inflation becomes persistent, people will cease to be surprised by inflation ('you cannot fool all of the people all of the time'), and any temporary decrease in unemployment will reverse.
- The relationship between inflation and monetary growth is not a direct one. However, inflation is a monetary phenomenon and can only be controlled through prudent monetary policy.
- Monetary policy should be directed towards the objective of achieving a stable price level; unemployment should be kept low by ensuring labour markets work effectively.
- An anti-inflation policy will cause less economic damage if people expect the policy to be followed and if there is a 'credible' framework for delivering monetary policy.
- Such a credible framework can be provided by an independent central bank with a well-defined objective.
- The current institutional arrangement for the conduct of monetary policy in the United Kingdom provides such a

framework.

- It would not be appropriate to create an independent fiscal authority because such an authority would have to balance the achievement of multiple objectives – a problem that is best settled in the political arena.
- While central banks do not generally target monetary growth directly when controlling inflation, it is nevertheless true that inflation is caused by excess monetary growth and can only be reduced by controlling monetary growth.

Money, Inflation and the Constitutional Position of the Central Bank

1   INTRODUCTION[1]
Geoffrey E. Wood

The importance given to monetary policy has increased greatly over the past decade or so: not only in Britain (but without doubt notably so here), but almost worldwide. In this volume are collected three papers, two by Milton Friedman and one by Charles Goodhart, which set out respectively the analysis and evidence behind the change, and how the framework of policy-making has altered in consequence of that change. This introductory essay aims neither to clarify nor bolster the papers by Milton Friedman and Charles Goodhart; doing so is unnecessary. Rather the aim is briefly to put them in their context in economic history and in the history of economic thought.[2]

Background: a historical perspective

Britain's inter-war unemployment experience (together with the much more serious unemployment problems, sometimes associated with political turmoil, in some other countries) greatly affected attitudes towards the economy. It led to a wartime White

---

1   I am indebted to Forrest Capie for his most useful comments on an earlier version of this introduction.

2   All page references to *The Counter-Revolution in Monetary Theory*, first published in 1970, and *Unemployment versus Inflation? An Evaluation of the Phillips Curve*, first published in 1975, are to the republished versions in this volume.

Paper on *Employment Policy* (1944), and to Beveridge's *Full Employment in a Free Society* (1944). Both of these wished a high level of employment to be maintained, with Beveridge setting a much more ambitious goal; he had tried to set out policies that would keep unemployment close to an average of 3 per cent. The interwar experience, in combination with the ambitions of these two publications, led even well into the post-war years to rapid relaxation of policy in response to even modest rises in unemployment. This concern to maintain low unemployment regardless of cost was undoubtedly behind the disastrous policies of the 1970s – demand was boosted, and there was little concern over what were remarkably high rates of growth of money, because unemployment was rising. Inflation, and the prospect of more inflation, was tolerated because it would bring down unemployment.

Or so it was thought. In his 1974 lecture (first published in 1975, and republished in this volume as the next chapter) Milton Friedman set out very clearly why that belief was erroneous, and showed what the intellectual origins of the error were.

The original truth which was later distorted into error was stated by Irving Fisher in 1926.[3] Fisher had observed that '... inflation was associated with low levels of unemployment and deflation with high levels' (see below, Friedman, ch. 2, p. 41). Why was this? Fisher's answer, briefly stated, is that an increase in nominal demand first stimulates output because every supplier thinks

---

3   Friedman's regard for his intellectual predecessors is worth remarking at this point. Unlike some economists, he is conscious that he is building on the work of predecessors, and is always careful to give those predecessors their due. He does that here, as he did some years earlier in his book *A Theory of the Consumption Function* (Princeton University Press for the National Bureau of Economic Research, 1957), in which he related his analysis of the consumption function to the work of Irving Fisher on the theory of the rate of interest.

there is an increase in demand for his product, an increase in *relative* demand, and only later realises that demand for all goods has gone up. In contrast, when in 1958 A. W. Phillips observed what came to be known as the 'Phillips curve', he treated changes in employment as starting off the process. His analysis, that is to say, started from the 'other end'. He started from the microeconomics of an individual market, and showed how an increase in demand would raise prices – in this case, wages. That is absolutely right for the individual market – an increase in demand raises the relative price, which in the labour market is the real wage of labour. But as Friedman points out, this is entirely unconnected (in principle – there is under some circumstances a qualification, discussed below, to the general statement) with money wages and money prices. The *real wage* $\frac{w}{p}$, which is the quantity that is determined in the labour market, can change without money wages (w) changing, if the general price level p changes; or, of course, if w and p both change in the same proportion then the real wage does not change (see below, Friedman, ch. 2, pp. 46–47).

It was perfectly understandable, given the intellectual climate when Phillips was writing, not to allow for this. If we are in circumstances such that after wage bargains are struck prices can change with no repercussions for wage bargains, Phillips was right to identify a curve that showed how a rise in prices (or in inflation) by lowering the real wage would lower unemployment. But the result depends on wage bargainers placidly allowing their bargains to be overturned.

Of course, they might. They might either temporarily or even permanently. It is an empirical matter – although if one found that people could be permanently 'fooled' by changes in the price level it would surely be troubling, as there is so much empirical work from other areas of economics which shows that relative prices, prices in real rather than money terms, affect behaviour.

What does the evidence from this area show? In his paper Friedman reviews the evidence up to the time he wrote and shows how the weight of it very much supports his view – people cannot be fooled by changes in prices for more than a short time, and changes in the inflation rate cannot affect permanently the level of unemployment. There has been much subsequent work on this, and the conclusion of it is massively in favour of the conclusion he reached in 1974. It is worth noting two very recent studies, one of the UK and one of the USA. Recollect that according to Fisher prices affect wages because people are not fooled by the price changes, so the curve he identified was the temporary one Friedman described. In the so-called Phillips curve, in contrast, the causation runs the other way, from wages to prices.

Recently Mills and Wood (2002) using UK data and Hess (1999), using US data, looked at this wage–price relationship. They found the identical result. To quote Hess: 'there is no systematic evidence that wages ... are helpful for predicting inflation'.

That finding is totally in contrast with the Phillips interpretation of the data, and fully consistent with the interpretation of Fisher and Friedman.[4]

Unemployment and the 'natural' rate

Friedman called the level of unemployment which was consistent

---

4   It must be emphasised that Phillips consistently opposed the interpretation of his work which claimed that the 'Phillips curve' presented a menu of inflation–unemployment combinations from which policymakers could choose their preferred positions.

with stable behaviour of the price level – either stable prices, or the price level moving in line with what people anticipated – the 'natural rate of unemployment'. He defined it (see below, ch. 2, p. 56) as 'That rate of unemployment which is consistent with existing real conditions in the labour market'. We can get away from it permanently by changing the 'real conditions' – by reducing, for example, the burdens people face when changing or seeking jobs. But we cannot get away from it permanently by changing the inflation rate, unless that rate keeps changing in an unpredictable way.

There are two often-made criticisms of that concept. The first is a relatively unsophisticated one, and arises simply from not knowing the origins of the term. The second, rather more subtle, queries whether there is only one 'natural rate'. These criticisms are considered in order.

The concept of the 'natural rate' has sometimes been attacked for its supposed implications. Some have taken it to mean that it corresponds to an inevitable level of unemployment, one that is desirable, perhaps optimal, and that those who use the concept are heartless and without concern for the plight of the unemployed. These objections arise simply from not knowing why Friedman used the term. As was remarked earlier, Friedman is sufficiently scholarly to pay due tribute to his predecessors. So he did with the term 'natural rate', for it was borrowed from Wicksell. It is an acknowledgement of an intellectual predecessor.

In his discussion of inflation and the rate of interest, Knut Wicksell (1899) used a term that was translated (by R. F. Kahn) as 'the natural rate of interest'. Wicksell introduced the term in the course of his discussion of inflation. In his analysis, if the central bank sets an interest rate away from the 'natural rate', then the necessary monetary consequences would lead to either continually rising or continually falling prices – to, in other words, a cumulative divergence of the price level from its starting point.

Friedman therefore chose the term 'natural rate of unemployment' as a labour market counterpart to Wicksell's natural rate of interest. Any attempt to move away from it by a monetary stimulus to demand (or, of course, a monetary contraction of demand) would lead to a cumulative divergence of the price level from its starting point. Unemployment *could* be moved permanently from that natural rate, but this could be done only by changing the working of the labour market, not by changing aggregate demand; by, in other words, changing the natural rate.[5]

A more subtle objection is that there may be more than one natural rate; that the equilibrium may not be unique. It actually requires a pretty restrictive set of assumptions to generate the uniqueness of equilibrium in a model of an economy. Indeed, there are some quite plausible models – where individuals face costs of search in finding, for example, the range of prices on offer for different goods – which make it rather likely that equilibrium will not be unique.[6]

---

5   Lars Jonung has drawn to my attention that Knut Wicksell, in a lecture on unemployment given in Malmö in 1901, described a level of unemployment with the same properties as Friedman's natural rate. Any attempt to deviate from it by monetary actions would ultimately lead only to cumulative price level change. This lecture survives only in note form.

6   It is also possible to show that if the supply of labour, given tastes, taxes, and so forth, depends not only on the real wage but also on wealth, then a changed price level without a change in the money supply will change the amount of labour supplied. This works throughout a channel now known as the wealth effect. It was explicit to varying degrees in the work of the classical economists, and completely so in the work of A. C. Pigou (e.g. 1917–18) and, notably, Patinkin (1956). The quantitative relevance of this effect is, however, generally thought to be small; and its analytical relevance is far from clear when the question at issue is the effect of a change in the money supply.

Suppose, then, we grant non-uniqueness to the natural rate of employment. If we do so in the present context, the appropriate response is surely 'so what?'. What follows *for monetary policy?* Suppose there are two natural rates. The lower one is presumably the more desirable. But even if we knew where it was, how would monetary policy get us there? What would happen to prices and to inflation? Thinking about these questions leads to the answer that we really do not know. Acknowledging the existence of multiple equilibria may well have implications for how severely one squeezes demand to reduce inflation, for it is possible that with a severe squeeze the economy would end up at an unnecessarily high level of unemployment. But noting that point is altogether different from denying that the appropriate aim of monetary policy is control of the price level. That is the true message of Friedman's 'natural rate' analysis.

Summarising so far, then, we have seen how inflation cannot have any permanent benign effect on unemployment. Indeed, it may well have a malign effect. Robert Barro (e.g. 1995) has provided us with formal, econometric, evidence that inflation reduces growth. This reinforced the insight of Lionel Robbins, writing in 1979: 'We only have to look around our own unhappy country, at the deterioration of industrial relations, the "real" profitability of enterprise, so concealed by historic cost accounting, and the general erosion of standards of public and private honesty, to see what can be done to a hitherto stable society by rates of inflation of the kind we have experienced in the past few years' (2001, p. 34).

No good comes of inflation. What causes it? How can we stop it?

Perspectives on inflation

It can be hard to grasp just how greatly ideas on money and inflation have changed. A good starting point for a perspective on this is 1959. In that year the Radcliffe Report was published. According to that report, monetary policy, in so far as it affected total demand, affected it through changing the ease of access to finance. To quote from that report: 'The authorities thus have to regard the structure of interest rates rather than the supply of money as the centre-piece of the monetary mechanism. This does not mean that the supply of money is unimportant, but that its control is incidental to interest rate policy.'

The Committee was concerned with what had immediate (or almost immediate) effects on the level of demand. The report's authors clearly believed that monetary policy had few, if any, such effects. Credit controls of various sorts, in contrast, did in their view have such effects. Hence attention was shifted from monetary policy to the role of credit restrictions and easings in producing short-term variations in demand. The long-run consequences of monetary actions were essentially neglected.

Inflation accelerated markedly in the 1960s, and became much more variable year to year than it had been (in Britain at any rate) in previous decades. One reaction to this was the introduction of a new framework for the conduct of monetary policy, 'Competition and Credit Control'. Put into effect in September 1971, it had two aims. There was a move away from direct controls on bank lending; aside from any other criticisms of such controls, they had been in place so long that they were being extensively evaded. The second aim was to move towards a market-oriented allocation of credit, to where credit was most desired rather than to where government thought was most deserving of it.

In the subsequent two years, to September 1973, the money supply expanded very rapidly. M3 grew at an annual average rate of about 26 per cent, and M1 at a rate of about 10 per cent. The economy grew rapidly and inflation started to accelerate. How much of this rapid acceleration in the economy was due to money is not easy to disentangle. There were *three* expansionary budgets between spring 1971 and spring 1972. Further, and more important, some of the monetary expansion is probably best viewed as 're-intermediation', the banks regaining a share of the lending they had lost during the years of credit controls. Interest rates were raised rapidly after inflation accelerated – but never enough to be above inflation; and credit controls were reintroduced.

In his 1970 paper (the first Wincott lecture, republished in this volume as the third chapter), Milton Friedman set out, and supported with evidence from a long historical period, the importance of money. Major monetary contractions cause major depressions – such a shock caused the Great Depression. And major monetary expansions cause major inflations.

To quote: 'It follows from what I have so far stated that *inflation is always and everywhere a monetary phenomenon* in the sense that it is and can be produced only by a more rapid increase in the quantity of money than in output' (see below, Friedman, ch. 3, p. 85, italics in original).

The quotation goes on: 'However, there are many possible reasons for monetary growth, including gold discoveries, financing of government spending, and financing of private spending.'

This raises an important point and, at the time of writing, one that is topical in the UK: it is touched on below.

As well as summarising the theory behind the money–inflation relationship (his survey started with Irving Fisher on the quantity theory of money), and citing applied work, Friedman drew attention to some particular episodes which help establish his propositions. These are worth highlighting, as they both illustrate an important aspect of scientific method and are relevant to current discussions. First, on the importance of money, and the dominance of monetary over fiscal policy in its effects on the economy, he looks at the USA in 1966 and 1967. In 1966 there was tight money and expansionary fiscal policy. Thus there was performed for us an experiment. Usually economists, when trying to see the effects of such policies, have trouble disentangling one from the other, for they usually move in the same direction in the same time period. Use of economic history helps us undertake that disentangling; modern economists, keen to use sophisticated statistical techniques, all too often forget how useful the study of individual episodes can be in solving one of the most tricky of statistical problems. So much for method.

What was the result of 'the experiment of 1966'? There was a significant slowing of economic activity in the first half of 1967, and, despite the preceding fiscal ease, only some nine months after the abrupt monetary easing which came in early 1967 did the economy accelerate again. A similar 'experiment' was performed in 1968 and 1969, but with the roles reversed. There was tight fiscal policy and easy money. The aim was to slow inflation. There was no sign of this starting to be achieved until some time after monetary policy was tightened from the end of 1968. Again the same conclusion emerges: monetary policy is what matters for inflation.

Just as in the case of the relationship between unemployment and inflation, since Milton Friedman gave this lecture there has been much work on the relationship between money growth and inflation. A recent, very useful and in the present context particularly relevant contribution to this literature is a paper by Mervyn King (2002).[7] In this article Mervyn King started out from an apparent paradox. As central banks, the issuers of money and controllers of monetary policy, have become more and more focused on the control of inflation, so the attention they appear to pay to the behaviour of the money supply seems to have declined. How can we understand this? It certainly does not result from any lack of evidence that money growth affects inflation. King provides a substantial amount of evidence from long runs of data to show that 'countries with faster growth rates of money experience higher inflation' (p. 163). This, he emphasises, is no mere correlation without causation; when the reasons for money growth are examined, it is clear that changes in the money supply without corresponding changes in demand for it do indeed cause inflation. It is true that, at the current time, central banks prefer to control money supply growth by controlling short-term interest rates, but King argues that the disappearance of money from economic models is more apparent than real and that models retain the property that it is money supply growth which ultimately affects prices. 'To understand the true role of money,' King also writes, 'a clear theoretical model is required and that model must allow for the central role of expectations' (p. 163). This is illustrated by examples from hyperinflations (that is to say, very rapid inflations).

Such periods are very helpful to the student of money, although of course to no one else. They are helpful because in those periods the monetary impulse, and associated inflation, is so substantial that all other variables become insignificant and the

---

7   Nelson (2002) also provides much evidence, concentrating on the role of a particular measure of the money stock, on this issue.

problem of seeing how much of what is going on is due to them simply disappears. The aspect of these episodes that King focused on to show the importance of expectations was that when people became convinced that money growth was going to slow, inflation started to slow, even though money growth had not yet done so. The reason for this is that the *expectation* of slowing money growth convinces people that they need not rush so frantically to spend the money before its value falls further, so the rate of price increase in turn starts to slow. King develops this point in various ways, and the point leads on to the paper in the present volume by Charles Goodhart. But before moving on, it is useful to take up another matter King raises. Is monetary policy impotent when the short-term interest rate is zero? This question was raised by Keynes in the 1930s, has current relevance in Japan, and possible relevance elsewhere given the low rates of inflation and hence interest rates in large parts of the developed world.

The argument that monetary policy is impotent is straightforward. When the money supply is increased at a zero interest rate, people just hold the money, for no return is given up by doing so. The contrary argument is that money is a substitute for many assets in addition to those which yield the short-term interest rate. It substitutes for a wide range of real and financial assets. Monetary expansion will influence the demand for those assets, and hence their yields, and in turn total spending in the economy, even when the short-term interest rate is zero.

Recent evidence, as King remarked, is mixed on this issue. But recent experience with very low interest rates is not all that abundant. Some years ago, two studies used long runs of data to look at the issue for, respectively, the USA and the UK. (Cagan and Schwartz, 1975; Mills and Wood, 1977). Both studies included the inter-war period in their data, and neither study found any evidence that people became willing passively to hold more and more increases in money as interest rates fell towards zero. This is certainly consistent with monetary policy retaining its influence at a low, possibly zero, short-term interest rate.

Expectations and central bank structure

Mervyn King noted the importance of expectations when seeking to understand the role of money in the economy. Expectations are also important in thinking both about central bank design and central bank conduct, the themes of the paper by Charles Goodhart in this collection.

Before going on to this paper it should be mentioned that Milton Friedman was an early contributor to this discussion also. On a variety of grounds he has for many years advocated the conduct of monetary policy by a pre-announced rule. There have been two strands to his argument. One was stated in the earlier of his two papers published here, and the other in the later paper.

As he explained in his 1970 lecture, one argument for guiding monetary policy by a rule is that doing so means that policy is right on average; and it is only on average that we can be confident about the link between money and inflation: 'It is precisely this leeway, this looseness in the relation, this lack of a mechanical one to one correspondence between changes in money and in income that is the primary reason why I have long favoured for the USA a quasi-automatic monetary policy under which the quantity of money would grow at a steady rate' (see below, Friedman, ch. 3, p. 89).

In the 1975 publication he set out the expectations-based reason for a rule. (The importance of expectations, of course, may

well underlie the looseness of the short-term relationship identified in the preceding quotation.) 'This analysis [in recognising the
importance of expectations] provides a different sort of intellectual background for a view some of us have held for a long time:
that it is a better approach to policy to say that you are going to co-
operate with the people and inform them of what you are doing, so
giving them a basis for their judgements, rather than trying to fool
them' (see below Friedman, ch. 2, p. 63). Friedman then went on to
a particular approach to the analysis of expectations, the approach
known as rational expectations. This approach presumes that people will form their expectations so as to avoid persistently being
wrong. They will, for example, try to anticipate government actions. In this, surely plausible, case, it becomes impossible persistently to fool people: 'What the analysis really suggests is that you
are fooling yourself, if you think that you can fool them' (p. 63).

These arguments have led in a variety of directions, but a basic
issue that has had to be confronted is what happens after a rule is
announced. How can we guarantee the government will stick to
its commitment? A way that has proved popular in the monetary
area is to set up an 'independent' central bank, charged with the
conduct of monetary policy. This does not of course make it impossible for the government to renege on its commitment, but it
does make it harder.

Interestingly, this proposal was discussed and rejected by
Milton Friedman in 1962 (reprinted in 1968: page references are
to the reprint). The starting point of his discussion was the question: '[W]hat kind of arrangements should a free society set up for
the control of monetary policy?'[8] Control over money, to quote

8   Friedman (1968), p. 173.

Friedman again, is 'a potent tool for controlling and shaping the economy'.[9] How can power be dispersed, as it should be to preserve freedom, in control over money? According to Friedman: 'The problem is to establish institutional arrangements that will enable government to exercise responsibility for money, yet will at the same time limit the power given to government and prevent the power from being used in ways that will tend to weaken rather than strengthen a free society.'[10]

It was in the context of addressing that problem that Friedman considered the concept of independence. He examined in turn an automatic commodity standard such as the gold standard, central bank independence, and finally legislative rules governing money growth. There is, he suggested, a 'trivial meaning' of the word 'independence' – when, within an agency of government, monetary policy is entrusted to some separate organisation which is subject to the head of that agency. Friedman then goes on to suggest 'a more basic meaning', which is that the central bank should be 'an independent branch of government, co-ordinate with the legislative, executive and judicial branches'.[11] It would, that is to say, have a mandate, analogous to the mandate given to the judiciary. It would carry out a law or laws passed by the government, and its operations could be interfered with by government only if the law – its mandate – were changed. Friedman goes on to suggest several grounds for doubting the efficacy of such a proposal, and to argue that a monetary rule is likely to be more effective.

This route has not been followed, and central banks have increasingly been granted 'independence'. And this brings us to the

9   Ibid., p. 174.
10   Ibid., p. 179
11   Ibid., p. 179.

final paper in this collection, that by Charles Goodhart, on 'The Constitutional Position of the Central Bank'.

As will be noted, the papers in this volume, and those discussed though not reprinted here, have all led us to the point where monetary policy is focused on the behaviour of the price level, and where that policy is guided by a rule. Charles Goodhart, in his Wincott lecture, considers the kind of institution that can best carry out such a policy, discusses some features of how it might do so, and the lessons the design of that institution may have for other institutions charged with economic responsibilities.

Goodhart defends central bank independence by two arguments. One strand of argument was particularly notable in New Zealand. There had been in that country increasingly detailed government interference in every aspect of economic life. There was, to quote Goodhart, 'constant political interference in the public sector'. (Such interference actually extended well beyond the public sector. There was, for example, guidance of bank lending towards politically favoured groups.) The Labour government that took office in New Zealand in 1984 had seen the harm such policies had done. In consequence, that government wished not only to rule such policies out for their term of office, but to set up institutional structures that would make it hard for such interference to resume. Sometimes the route chosen was privatisation. On other occasions the route was to specify the objectives in a contract between senior officials in the ministries (or other public sector bodies) concerned, and then leave them to get on with achieving these agreed objectives. The policy favoured for the Reserve Bank of New Zealand (RBNZ) fell naturally into that latter group, and it ended up looking markedly like the current form of the Bank of England, with an inflation target set by government but the bank left to achieve it. (The RBNZ has no monetary policy committee; the policy decisions are the sole responsibility of its governor.[12])

The second strand of argument leading to an independent central bank is that only by such independence, along with a clear mandate, can a stable monetary rule, announced in advance and then adhered to, be if not guaranteed then made more likely.

A full description of the arguments for this can be found in Charles Goodhart's paper, so they can be treated briefly here. The strong form of the argument is that once a monetary policy rule has been announced, there is an incentive for politicians to deviate from it to stimulate the economy so as to win an election. But as the timing of the effects of monetary policy is so uncertain such an effort would be unlikely to be fruitful. A much more likely source of problems is the difficulty that has beset UK monetary policy for many years (indeed, just this was noted earlier in the discussion of the errors of the 1970s): delay in tightening in the hope that things would go well of their own accord. (This delay in part reflects the power of concentrated groups – the lobby for low interest rates is much more effective than the rather more diffuse body of savers, who have at least some reasons for doubting the benefits of low rates.)

Now, what is this independent central bank going to do? Charles Goodhart rejects Milton Friedman's objection to an independent central bank with a mandate to hit an inflation target on the grounds that although the central bank's control of inflation is imperfect, an aspect of Friedman's objection, many individuals have their performance judged by the behaviour of things over which their control is imperfect.

---

12 Those wishing a detailed description and analysis of the development of the Reserve Bank of New Zealand can find an overview, and further references, in Wood (1994).

That is undoubtedly true. Whether it is decisive is something about which there is probably still some dispute; but be that as it may, there would certainly be agreement that, so long as the central bank continues (as Mervyn King urged it should in his paper discussed above) to pay heed to measures of the money supply, a framework of inflation targets with attention to the money supply is certainly satisfactory.[13]

Having set out a framework for the conduct of monetary policy, Charles Goodhart then turns to a range of related issues. Should we have an independent fiscal authority, charged with carrying out a pre-announced fiscal rule? The idea has attractions, but, as he points out, there are problems in framing the rule, and fiscal policy may involve the kind of trade-offs where decision-making by elected politicians is appropriate.

In his discussion of trade-offs, Charles Goodhart notes an important, but nevertheless generally not discussed, feature of the current British monetary control framework. Conflicts between the objectives of stable prices and stable output are in the long run absent, but in the short run reducing inflation is indeed likely to require reducing output growth (or possibly even output). This is, however, only a problem leading to a trade-off if a shock has driven output and inflation in opposite directions. In the face of a demand shock, which would move output and inflation in the same direction, monetary policy faces no conflict. Further, if a shock has

---

13 Another reason for distancing monetary policy from government comes from the possibility of an increase in wages coming not from an increase in demand, but from a one-off exertion of union power. It is likely to be easier for a central bank than for a government to resist pressure to accommodate that by a monetary expansion so as to prevent the otherwise inevitable rise in unemployment: a rise that could, in any case, only be delayed by expansionary monetary policy, as the Friedman papers show us.

driven inflation outside its target range, a dialogue can open up between the Governor of the Bank of England and the Chancellor of the Exchequer over how fast to get back on target, thus introducing some political input into a process where there are trade-offs.[14]

Conclusion

The three papers reprinted in this collection, although widely separated in the times in which they were written, are not only important but coherent and intimately linked. They show the role of money in inflation, demonstrate that inflation control is the only appropriate target for monetary policy, and set out the institutional framework in which monetary policy appropriate for the production of a good approximation to price stability can be achieved. They are clear, informative and judicious. These papers will be of interest to everyone interested in the role of monetary policy and in the constitutional framework for monetary stability. That, surely, should be a very wide audience.

References

Barro, R. (1995), 'Inflation and Economic Growth', *Bank of England Quarterly Bulletin*, May.

Beveridge, W. H. (1944), *Full Employment in a Free Society*, Allen & Unwin.

Cagan, P., & Schwartz, A. J. (1975), 'Has the Growth of Money Substitutes Hindered Monetary Policy?', *Journal of Money*

---

14 There is also room for such political input, albeit by a different route, in the Reserve Bank of New Zealand constitution. See Wood (1994) for details on this.

Credit and Banking 7 (2), May: 137–59.

Employment Policy (1944), Cmnd 6527, May.

Friedman, M. (1962), 'Should there be an Independent Monetary Authority?', in L. B. Yeager (ed.), *In Search of a Monetary Constitution*, Harvard University Press, Boston, Mass.

Hess, G. (1999), 'Does wage inflation cause price inflation?', Bradley Policy Research Centre Shadow Open Market Committee Policy Statement, and Position Papers 26–7, September: 11–24.

King, Mervyn (2002), 'No money, no inflation: the role of money in the economy', *Bank of England Quarterly Bulletin*, August.

Mills, T. C., & Wood, G. E. (2002), 'Wages and Prices in the UK', *Applied Economics* 34: 2143–9.

Mills T. C., & Wood, G. E. (1977), 'Money Substitutes and Monetary Policy in the UK 1922–1976', *European Economic Review*, vol. 10: 19–36.

Nelson, Edward (2002), 'Direct Effects of Base Money on Aggregate Demand', *Journal of Monetary Economics* 49: 687–708.

Patinkin, D. (1956), *Money, Interest and Prices*, Harper and Row, New York.

Pigou, A. C. (1917–18), 'The Value of Money', *Quarterly Journal of Economics* XXXII: 162–83.

Radcliffe Report (1959), Committee on the Working of the Monetary System, Cmnd 827, August.

Robbins, Lionel (2001), 'Objectives of Monetary Policy Past and Present', in *Policy Makers on Policy*, F. H. Capie & G. E. Wood (eds), Routledge, London.

Wicksell, K. (1899), *Interest and Prices* (trans. R. F. Kahn, 1936), Macmillan, London.

Wood, G. E. (1994), 'A Pioneers' Bank', *Central Banking*, August.

2 UNEMPLOYMENT VERSUS INFLATION? AN EVALUATION OF THE PHILLIPS CURVE

Milton Friedman

Fisher and Philips

The discussion of the Phillips curve started with truth in 1926, proceeded through error some 30 years later, and by now has returned back to 1926 and to the original truth. That is about 50 years for a complete circuit. You can see how technological development has speeded up the process of both producing and dissipating ignorance.

I choose the year 1926 not at random but because in that year Irving Fisher published an article in the *International Labour Review* under the title 'A Statistical Relation between Unemployment and Price Changes'.[1]

The Fisher approach

Fisher's article dealt with precisely the same empirical phenomenon that Professor A. W. Phillips analysed in his celebrated article in *Economica* some 32 years later.[2] Both were impressed with the empirical observation that inflation tended to be associated with

1   June 1926, pp. 785–92. It was reprinted in the *Journal of Political Economy*, March/ April, 1973, pp. 496–502.

2   'The Relation between Unemployment and the Rate of Change of Money Wage Rates in the United Kingdom, 1861–1957', *Economica*, November 1958, pp. 283– 99.

low levels of unemployment and deflation with high levels. One amusing item in Fisher's article from a very different point of view is that he starts out by saying that he has been so deeply interested in this subject that 'during the last three years in particular I have had at least one computer in my office almost constantly at work on this project'.[3] Of course what he meant was a human being operating a calculating machine.

There was, however, a crucial difference between Fisher's analysis and Phillips', between the truth of 1926 and the error of 1958, which had to do with the direction of causation. Fisher took *the rate of change of prices* to be the independent variable that set the process going. In his words,

> When the dollar is losing value, or in other words when the
> price level is rising, a business man finds his receipts rising
> as fast, on the average, as this general rise of prices, but not
> his expenses, because his expenses consist, to a large extent,
> of things which are contractually fixed ... Employment is
> then stimulated – for a time at least.[4]

To elaborate his analysis and express it in more modern terms, let anything occur that produces a higher level of spending – or, more precisely, a higher rate of increase in spending than was anticipated. Producers would at first interpret the faster rate of increase in spending as an increase in real demand for their product. The producers of shoes, hats, or coats would discover that apparently there was an increase in the amount of goods they could sell at pre-existing prices. No one of them would know at first whether the change was affecting him in particular or whether it was general. In

3   Fisher, op. cit., p. 786.
4   Ibid., p. 787.

the first instance, each producer would be tempted to expand output, as Fisher states, and also to allow prices to rise. But at first much or most of the unanticipated increase in nominal demand (i.e. demand expressed in £s) would be absorbed by increases (or faster increases) in employment and output rather than by increases (or faster increases) in prices. Conversely, for whatever reason, let the rate of spending slow down, or rise less rapidly than was anticipated, and each individual producer would in the first instance interpret the slow-down at least partly as reflecting something peculiar to him. The result would be partly a slow-down in output and a rise in unemployment and partly a slow-down in prices.

Fisher was describing a *dynamic* process arising out of fluctuations in the rate of spending about some average trend or norm. He went out of his way to emphasise the importance of distinguishing between 'high and low prices on the one hand and the rise and fall of prices on the other'.[5] He put it that way because he was writing at a time when a stable level of prices was taken to be the norm. Were he writing today, he would emphasise the distinction between the rate of inflation and changes in the rate of inflation. (And perhaps some future writer will have to emphasise the difference between the second and the third derivatives!) The important distinction – and it is quite clear that this is what Fisher had in mind – is between *anticipated* and *unanticipated* changes.

The Phillips approach

Professor Phillips' approach was from exactly the opposite

---

5   Ibid., p. 788.

Figure 1

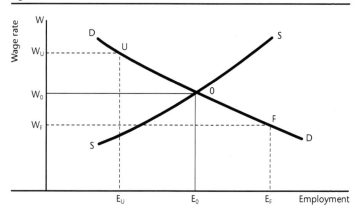

direction. He took the level of *employment* to be the independent variable that set the process going. He treated the rate of change of wages as the dependent variable. His argument was a very simple analysis – I hesitate to say simple-minded, but so it has proved – in terms of *static supply* and demand conditions. He said:

> When the demand for a commodity or service is high relatively to the supply of it we expect the price to rise, the rate of rise being greater the greater the excess demand ... It seems plausible that this principle should operate as one of the factors determining the rate of change of money wage rates, which are the price of labour services.[6]

Phillips' approach is based on the usual (*static*) demand and supply curves as illustrated in Figure 1. At the point of intersection, o, the market is in equilibrium at the wage rate W_0, with

---

6   Phillips, op. cit., p. 283.

Figure 2

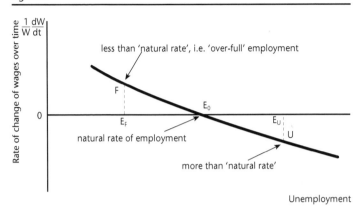

the amount of labour employed E_0 equal to the amount of labour demanded. Unemployment is zero – which is to say, as measured, equal to 'frictional' or 'transitional' unemployment, or to use the terminology I adopted some years ago from Wicksell, at its 'natural' rate. At this point, says Phillips, there is no upward pressure on wages. Consider instead the point F, where the quantity of labour demanded is higher than the quantity supplied. There is over-employment, wages at W_F are below the equilibrium level, and there will be upward pressure on them. At point U, there is unemployment, W_U is above the equilibrium wage rate and there is downward pressure. The larger the discrepancy between the quantity of labour demanded and the quantity supplied, the stronger the pressure and hence the more rapidly wages will rise or fall.

Phillips translated this analysis into an observable relation by plotting the level of unemployment on one axis, and the rate

Figure 3

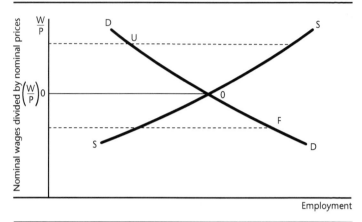

of change of wages over time on the other, as in Figure 2. Point E_0 corresponds to point o in Figure 1. Unemployment is at its 'natural' rate so wages are stable (or in a growing economy, rising at a rate equal to the rate of productivity growth). Point F corresponds to 'over-full' employment, so wages are rising; point U to unemployment, so wages are falling.

Fisher talked about price changes, Phillips about wage changes, but I believe that for our purpose that is not an important distinction. Both Fisher and Phillips took it for granted that wages are a major component of total cost and that prices and wages would tend to move together. So both of them tended to go very readily from rates of wage change to rates of price change and I shall do so as well.

The fallacy in Phillips

Phillips' analysis seems very persuasive and obvious, yet it is utterly fallacious. It is fallacious because no economic theorist has ever asserted that the demand and supply of labour were functions of the *nominal* wage rate (i.e. wage rate expressed in £s). Every economic theorist from Adam Smith to the present would have told you that the vertical axis in Figure 1 should refer not to the *nominal* wage rate but to the *real* wage rate.

But once you label the vertical axis $\frac{W}{P}$ as in Figure 3, the graph has nothing to say about what is going to happen to *nominal wages* or prices. There is not even any *prima facie* presumption that it has anything to say. For example, consider point o in Figure 3. At that level of employment, there is neither upward nor downward pressure on the real wage. But that real wage can remain constant with W and P separately *constant*, or with W and P each *rising* at the rate of 10 per cent a year, or *falling* at the rate of 10 per cent a year, or doing anything else, provided both change at the *same* rate.

The Keynesian confusion between nominal and real wages

How did a sophisticated mind like Phillips' – and he was certainly a highly sophisticated and subtle economist – come to confuse nominal wages with real wages? He was led to do so by the general intellectual climate that had been engendered by the Keynesian revolution. From this point of view, the essential element of the Keynesian revolution was the assumption that prices are highly rigid relative to output so that a change in demand of the kind considered by Fisher would be reflected almost entirely in *output* and very little in prices. The price level could be regarded as an institutional datum. The simple way to interpret Phillips is that he was therefore assuming the change in nominal wages to be equal to the change in real wages.

But that is not really what he was saying. What he was saying was slightly more sophisticated. It was that changes in *anticipated* nominal wages were equal to changes in *anticipated* real wages. There were two components of the Keynesian system that were essential to his construction: first, the notion that prices are rigid in the sense that people in planning their behaviour do not allow for the possibility that the price level might change, and hence regard a change in nominal wages or nominal prices as a change in real wages and real prices; second, that real wages *ex post* could be altered by *unanticipated* inflation. Indeed the whole Keynesian argument for the possibility of a full employment policy arose out of the supposition that it was possible to get workers (at least in the 1930s when Keynes wrote *The General Theory)* to accept lower real wages produced by inflation that they would not have accepted in the direct form of a reduction in nominal wages.[7]

These two components imply a sharp distinction between *anticipated* nominal and real wages and *actual* nominal and real wages. In the Keynesian climate of the time, it was natural for Phillips to take this distinction for granted, and to regard anticipated nominal and real wages as moving together.

---

7   J. M. Keynes, *The General Theory of Employment, Interest, and Money* (Macmillan, 1936): 'Whilst workers will usually resist a reduction of money wages, it is not their practice to withdraw their labour whenever there is a rise in the price of wage-goods' (p. 9). ' … The workers, though unconsciously, are instinctively more reasonable economists than the classical school … They resist reductions of money-wages … whereas they do not resist reductions of real wages' (p. 14). '… Since no trade union would dream of striking on every occasion of a rise in the cost of living, they do not raise the obstacle to any increase in aggregate employment attributed to them by the classical school' (p. 15).

I do not criticise Phillips for doing this. Science is possible only because at any one time there is a body of conventions or views or ideas that are taken for granted and on which scientists build. If each individual writer were to go back and question all the premises that underlie what he is doing, nobody would ever get anywhere. I believe that some of the people who have followed in his footsteps deserve much more criticism than he does for not noting the importance of this theoretical point once it was pointed out to them.

At any rate, it was this general intellectual climate that led Phillips to think in terms of nominal rather than real wages. The intellectual climate was also important in another direction. The Keynesian system, as everybody knows, is incomplete. It lacks an equation. A major reason for the prompt and rapid acceptance of the Phillips curve approach was the widespread belief that it provided the missing equation that connected the real system with the monetary system. In my opinion, this belief is false. What is needed to complete the Keynesian system is an equation that determines the equilibrium price level. But the Phillips curve deals with the relation between a rate of change of prices or wages and the level of unemployment. It does not determine an equilibrium price level. At any rate, the Phillips curve was widely accepted and was seized on immediately for policy purposes.[8] It is still widely

---

8   For example, Albert Rees, 'The Phillips Curve as a Menu for Policy Choices', *Economica*, August 1970, pp. 227–38, explicitly considers the objections to a stable Phillips curve outlined below, yet concludes that there remains a trade-off that should be exploited. He writes: 'The strongest policy conclusion I can draw from the expectations literature is that the policy makers should not attempt to operate at a single point on the Phillips curve … Rather, they should permit fluctuations in unemployment within a band' (p. 238).

used for this purpose as supposedly describing a 'trade-off', from a policy point of view, between inflation and unemployment.

It was said that what the Phillips curve means is that we are faced with a choice. If we choose a low level of inflation, say, stable prices, we shall have to reconcile ourselves to a high level of unemployment. If we choose a low level of unemployment, we shall have to reconcile ourselves to a high rate of inflation.

Reaction against the Keynesian system

Three developments came along in this historical account to change attitudes and to raise some questions.

One was the general theoretical reaction against the Keynesian system which brought out into the open the fallacy in the original Phillips curve approach of identifying nominal with real wages.

The second development was the failure of the Phillips curve relation to hold for other bodies of data. Fisher had found it to hold for the United States for the period before 1925; Phillips had found it to hold for Britain for a long period. But, lo and behold, when people tried it for any other place they never obtained good results. Nobody was able to construct a decent empirical Phillips curve for other circumstances. I may be exaggerating a bit – no doubt there are other successful cases; but certainly a large number of attempts were unsuccessful.

The third and most recent development is the emergence of 'stagflation', which rendered somewhat ludicrous the confident statements that many economists had made about 'trade-offs', based on empirically-fitted Phillips curves.

Short- and long-run Phillips curves

The empirical failures and the theoretical reaction produced an attempt to rescue the Phillips curve approach by distinguishing a short-run from a long-run Phillips curve. Because both potential employers and potential employees envisage an implicit or explicit employment contract covering a fairly long period, both must guess in advance what real wage will correspond to a given nominal wage. Both therefore must form anticipations about the future price level. The real wage rate that is plotted on the vertical axis of the demand and supply curve diagram is thus not the *current* real wage but the *anticipated* real wage. If we suppose that anticipations about the price level are slow to change, while the nominal wage can change rapidly and is known with little time-lag, we can, for *short* periods, revert essentially to Phillips' original formulation, except that the equilibrium position is no longer a constant nominal wage, but a nominal wage changing at the same rate as the anticipated rate of change in prices (plus, for a growing economy, the anticipated rate of change in productivity). Changes in demand and supply will then show up first in a changed rate of change of nominal wages, which will mean also in anticipated real wages. Current prices may adjust as rapidly as or more rapidly than wages, so real wages *actually* received may move in the opposite direction from nominal wages, but *anticipated* real wages will move in the same direction.

One way to put this in terms of the Phillips curve is to plot on the vertical axis not the change in nominal wages but that change minus the anticipated rate of change in prices, as in the revised Figure 2, where $(\frac{1}{P} \frac{dP}{dt})^*$, standing for the anticipated rate of change in prices, is subtracted from $\frac{1}{W} \frac{dW}{dt}$. This curve now tells a story much more like Fisher's original story than Phillips'. Suppose, to start

Figure 2 revised

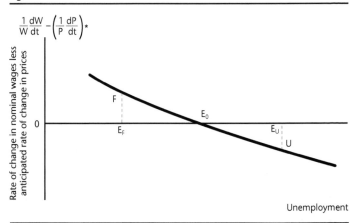

with, the economy is at point E_O, with both prices and wages stable (abstracting from growth). Suppose something, say, a monetary expansion, starts nominal aggregate demand growing, which in turn produces a rise in prices and wages at the rate of, say, 2 per cent per year. Workers will initially interpret this as a rise in their real wage – because they still anticipate constant prices – and so will be willing to offer more labour (move up their supply curve), i.e. employment grows and unemployment falls. Employers may have the same anticipations as workers about the general price level, but they are more directly concerned about the price of the products they are producing and far better informed about that. They will initially interpret a rise in the demand for and price of their product as a rise in its relative price and as implying a fall in the real wage rate they must pay measured in terms of their product. They will therefore be willing to hire more labour (move down their demand curve). The combined result is a movement, say, to point F, which corresponds with 'over-full' employment, with nominal wages rising at 2 per cent per year.

But, as time passes, both employers and employees come to recognise that prices *in general* are rising. As Abraham Lincoln said, 'You can fool all of the people some of the time, you can fool some of the people all of the time, but you can't fool all of the people all of the time.' As a result, they raise their estimate of the anticipated rate of inflation, which reduces the rate of rise of anticipated real wages, and leads you to slide down the curve back ultimately to the point Eo. There is thus a *short-run* 'trade-off' between inflation and unemployment, but *no long-run* 'trade-off'.

By incorporating price anticipations into the Phillips curve as I have just done, I have implicitly begged one of the main issues in the recent controversy about the Phillips curve. Thanks to recent experience of 'stagflation' plus theoretical analysis, everyone now admits that the apparent short-run Phillips curve is misleading and seriously overstates the *short*-run trade-off, but many are not willing to accept the view that the *long*-run trade-off is *zero*.

We can examine this issue by using a different way of incorporating price anticipations into the Phillips curve. Figure 4 keeps the rate of change of nominal wages on the vertical axis but contains a series of different curves, one for each anticipated rate of growth of wages. To put it algebraically, instead of writing the Phillips curve relation as

(1) $\frac{1}{W}\frac{dW}{dt} - (\frac{1}{P}\frac{dP}{dt})^* = f(U),$

where U is unemployment, we can write it in more general form as

Figure 4

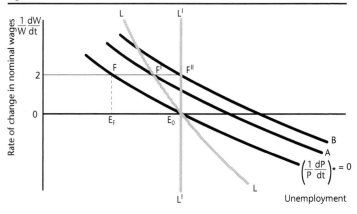

(2) $\qquad \frac{1}{W} \frac{dW}{dt} = f\left[U, \left(\frac{1}{P} \frac{dP}{dt}\right)\star\right]$

Now suppose something occurs to put the economy at point F at which wages are rising at 2 per cent a year and unemployment is less than the natural rate. Then, as people adjust their expectations of inflation, the short-run Phillips curve will shift upwards and the final resting place would be on that short-run Phillips curve at which the anticipated rate of inflation equals the current rate. The issue now becomes whether that Phillips curve is like A, so that the long-run curve is negatively sloping, like LL, in which case an anticipated rate of inflation of 2 per cent will still reduce the level of unemployment, though not by as much as an unanticipated rate of 2 per cent, or whether it is like B, so that the long-run curve is *vertical*, that is, unemployment is the *same* at a 2 per cent anticipated rate of inflation as at a zero per cent anticipated rate.

No long-run money illusion

In my Presidential Address to the American Economic Association seven years ago, I argued that the long-run Phillips curve was vertical, largely on the grounds I have already sketched here: in effect, the absence of any long-run money illusion.[9] At about the same time, Professor E. S. Phelps, now of Columbia University, offered the same hypothesis, on different though related grounds.[10] This hypothesis has come to be called the 'accelerationist' hypothesis or the 'natural rate' hypothesis. It has been called accelerationist because a policy of trying to hold unemployment below the horizontal intercept of the long-run vertical Phillips curve must lead to an *accelerated* inflation.

Suppose, beginning at point E_0, on Figure 4, when nobody anticipated any inflation, it is decided to aim at a lower unemployment level, say E_F. This can be done initially by producing an inflation of 2 per cent, as shown by moving along the Phillips curve corresponding to anticipations of no inflation. But, as we have seen, the economy will not stay at F because people's anticipations will shift, and if the rate of inflation were kept at 2 per cent, the economy would be driven back to the level of unemployment it started with. The only way unemployment can be kept below the 'natural rate' is by an *ever-accelerating* inflation, which always keeps current inflation ahead of anticipated inflation. Any resemblance between that analysis and what you in Britain have been observing in practice is not coincidental: what recent British governments have tried to do is to keep unemployment below

9 'The Role of Monetary Policy', *American Economic Review*, March 1968, pp. 1–17.
10 'Money Wage Dynamics and Labour Market Equilibrium', in E. S. Phelps (ed.), *Microeconomic Foundations of Employment and Inflation Theory*, Norton Press, New York, 1970.

the natural rate, and to do so they have had to accelerate inflation – from 3.9 per cent in 1964 to 16.0 per cent in 1974, according to your official statistics.[11, 12]

Misunderstandings about the 'natural rate' of unemployment

The hypothesis came to be termed the 'natural rate' hypothesis because of the emphasis on the natural rate of unemployment. The term 'the natural rate' has been misunderstood. It does not refer to some *irreducible minimum* of unemployment. It refers rather to that rate of employment which is consistent with the *existing* real *conditions* in the labour market. It can be lowered by removing obstacles in the labour market, by reducing friction. It can be raised by introducing additional obstacles. The purpose of the concept is to separate the monetary from the non-monetary aspects of the employment situation – precisely the same purpose that Wicksell had in using the word 'natural' in connection with the rate of interest.

In the past few years, a large number of statistical studies have investigated the question of whether the long-run Phillips curve is or is not vertical. That dispute is still in train.

Most of the statistical tests were undertaken by rewriting Equation (2) in the form:

$$(3) \qquad \frac{1}{W} \frac{dW}{dt} = a + b \left(\frac{1}{P} \frac{dP}{dt} \right)^{\star} + f(U)$$

11 United Kingdom General Index of Retail Prices, *Department of Employment Gazette*.

12 It is worth noting that the annual rate of inflation peaked at over 26 per cent and the annualised monthly rate at over 66 per cent after this paper was originally published.

or

$$\frac{1}{P} \frac{dP}{dt} = a + b\left(\frac{1}{P}\frac{dP}{dt}\right)^{\star} + f(U),$$

where the left-hand side was either the rate of change of wages or the rate of change of prices. The question then asked was what is the value of b.[13] The original Phillips curve essentially assumed b = 0; the acceleration hypothesis set b equal to 1. The authors of the various tests I am referring to used observed data, mostly time-series data, to estimate the numerical value of b.[14] Almost every such test has come out with a numerical value of b less than 1, implying that there is a long-run 'trade-off'.[15] However, there are a number of difficulties with these tests, some on a rather superficial level, others on a much more fundamental level.

One obvious statistical problem is that the statistically fitted

---

13 This is the coefficient on the anticipated rate of inflation, that is, the percentage point change in the current rate of change in wages or in prices that would result from a 1 percentage point change in the anticipated rate of inflation.

14 I might note as an aside that one much-noticed attempt along these lines was contained in lectures given in Britain by Robert Solow a few years ago (*Price Expectations and the Behaviour of the Price Level*, Manchester University Press, 1969). Unfortunately, his test has a fatal flaw which renders it irrelevant to the current issue. In order to allow for costs as well as demand, he included on the right-hand side of an equation like Equation (3) the rate of change of wages, and, on the left-hand side, the rate of change of prices. In such an equation, there is no reason to expect b to be unity even on the strictest acceleration hypothesis, because the equation is then an equation to determine what happens to the margin between prices and wages. Let the anticipated rate of inflation rise by one percentage point, but the rate of change of wages be held constant, and any resulting rise in prices raises the excess of prices over costs and so stimulates output. Hence, in Solow's equation, the strict acceleration hypothesis would imply that b was less than 1.

15 A succinct summary of these studies is in S. J. Turnovsky, 'On the Role of Inflationary Expectations in a Short-Run Macro-Economic Model', *Economic Journal*, June 1974, pp. 317–37, especially pp. 326–27.

curves have not been the same for different periods of fit and have produced very unreliable extrapolations for periods subsequent to the period of fit. So it looks very much as if the statistical results are really measuring a short-term relationship despite the objective. The key problem here is that, in order to make the statistical test, it is necessary to have some measure of the anticipated rate of inflation. Hence, every such test is a joint test of the accelerationist hypothesis and a particular hypothesis about the formation of anticipations.

The adaptive expectations hypothesis

Most of these statistical tests embody the so-called adaptive expectations hypothesis, which has worked well in many problems. It states that anticipations are revised on the basis of the difference between the current rate of inflation and the anticipated rate. If the anticipated rate was, say, 5 per cent but the current rate 10 per cent, the anticipated rate will be revised upward by some fraction of the difference between 10 and 5. As is well known, this implies that the anticipated rate of inflation is an exponentially weighted average of past rates of inflation, the weights declining as one goes back in time.

Even on their own terms, then, these results are capable of two different interpretations. One is that the long-run Phillips curve is not vertical but has a negative slope. The other is that this has not been a satisfactory method of evaluating people's expectations for this purpose.

A somewhat more subtle statistical problem with these equations is that, if the accelerationist hypothesis is correct, the results are either estimates of a short-run curve or are statistically unstable. Suppose the true value of b is unity. Then when current inflation equals anticipated inflation, which is the definition of a long-run curve, we have that

$$(4) \qquad f(U) = -a.$$

This is the vertical long-run Phillips curve with the value of U that satisfies it being the natural rate of unemployment. Any other values of U reflect either short-term equilibrium positions or a stochastic component in the natural rate. But the estimation process used, with $\frac{1}{P}\frac{dP}{dt}$ on the left-hand side, treats different observed rates of unemployment as if they were exogenous, as if they could persist indefinitely. There is simply no way of deriving Equation (4) from such an approach. In effect, the implicit assumption that unemployment can take different values begs the whole question raised by the accelerationist hypothesis. On a statistical level, this approach requires putting U, or a function of U, on the left-hand side, not $\frac{1}{P}\frac{dP}{dt}$.

Rational expectations

A still more fundamental criticism has recently been made by a number of economists in the United States. This criticism has its origin in an important article by John Muth on rational expectations. The rational expectations approach has been applied to the problem in recent articles by Robert Lucas of Carnegie-Mellon (later Chicago), Tom Sargent of the University of Minnesota, and a number of others.[16]

16 John Muth, 'Rational Expectations and the Theory of Price Movements', *Econometrica, July* 1961, pp. 315–35; Robert E. Lucas, 'Econometric Testing of the Natural

Figure 5

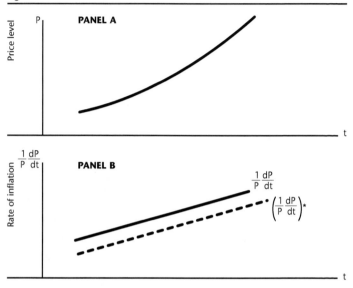

This criticism is that you cannot take seriously the notion that people form anticipations on the basis of a weighted average of past experience with fixed weights – or any other scheme that is inconsistent with the way inflation is really being generated. For

Rate Hypothesis', in Otto Eckstein (ed.), *The Econometrics of Price Determination Conference*, Board of Governors of the Federal Reserve System and Social Science Research Council, Washington, 1972, 'Econometric Policy Evaluation: A Critique', Carnegie-Mellon University Working Paper, 1973, 'Some International Evidence on Output- Inflation Tradeoffs', *American Economic Review*, June 1973, pp. 326–34; Thomas J. Sargent, 'Rational Expectations, the Real Rate of Interest, and the "Natural" Rate of Unemployment', *Brookings Papers on Economic Activity*, Vol. 2, 1973, pp. 429–72; and Thomas J. Sargent and Neil Wallace, '"Rational" Expectations, the Optimal Money Instrument and the Optimal Money Supply Rule', *Journal of Political Economy*, April 1974.

example, let us suppose that the current course of the price level is the one drawn on panel A of Figure 5, that inflation is accelerating. With a fixed exponential weighting pattern (with weights summing to unity) the anticipated rate of inflation will always be lagging behind, as in Panel B. But people who are forming anticipations are not fools – or at least some of them are not. They are not going to *persist* in being wrong. And more generally they are not going to base their anticipations solely on the past history of prices. Is there anybody in this room whose anticipation of inflation next year will be independent of the result of the coming British elections ? That is not reported in the past record of prices. Will it be independent of policies announced by the parties that come into power, and so on ? Therefore, said Muth, we should assume that people form their anticipations on the basis of a correct economic theory: not that they are right in *each individual* case but that over any long period they *will on the average* be right. Sometimes this will lead to the formation of anticipations on the basis of adaptive expectations, but by no means always.

If you apply that idea to the present problem it turns out that, if the true world is one in which people form expectations on a rational basis so that on the average they are right, then assuming that they form expectations by averaging the past with fixed weights will yield a value of b in equation (3) less than unity even though the true value is unity.

Consider a world in which there is a vertical long-run Phillips curve and in which people form their expectations rationally, so that on the average, over a long period, their expectations are equal to what happens. In such a world, the statistician comes along and estimates equation (3) on the assumption that people form their anticipations by averaging past experience with fixed weights. What will he find? It turns out that he will find that b is less than 1. Of course, this possibility does not prove that the statistical tests incorporating adaptive expectations are wrong but only provides an alternative interpretation of their results.

In a series of very interesting and important papers, Lucas and Sargent[17] have explored the implication of the rational expectations hypothesis and have tried to derive empirical tests of the slope of the long-run Phillips curve without the possibly misleading assumption of adaptive expectations.

Their empirical tests use a different kind of information. For example, one implication of a rational expectations hypothesis is that, in a country in which prices have fluctuated a great deal, expectations will respond to changes in the current rate of inflation much more rapidly than in a country in which prices have been relatively stable. It follows that the observed short-run Phillips curve will be steeper in the first country than in the second. Comparisons among countries in this way, as well as other tests, seem so far entirely consistent with what any reasonable man must surely expect: which is that, *since you can't fool all the people all the time, the true long-run Phillips curve is vertical*.

Implications for theory and policy

It is worth noting how far-reaching are the implications of this view not only for the Phillips curve problem but also for policy.

One very strong and very important implication for policy is that, if you treat people as forming expectations on a rational basis, no fixed rule of monetary or fiscal policy will enable you to

---

17   Footnote 18, p. 75.

achieve anything other than the natural rate of unemployment. And you can see why. Because – to go back to my initial Phillips curve analysis – the only way in which you ever get a reduction of unemployment is through *unanticipated* inflation.

If the government follows any fixed rule whatsoever, *so long as the people know it*, they will be able to take it into account. And consequently you cannot achieve an unemployment target other than the natural rate by any fixed rule. The only way you can do so is by continually being cleverer than all the people, by continually making up *new* rules and using them for a while until people catch up with them. Then you must invent a new set of rules. That is not a very promising possibility.

This analysis provides a different sort of intellectual background for a view that some of us have held for a long time: that it is a better approach to policy to say that you are going to co-operate with the people and inform them of what you are doing, so giving them a basis for their judgements, rather than trying to fool them. What the Sargent/Lucas argument and analysis really suggests is that you are fooling yourself if you think that you can fool them.

That is about where the present state of the argument is. I might summarise by saying that there is essentially no economist any longer who believes in the naive Phillips curve of the kind originally proposed. The argument has shifted now to a second level, where everybody agrees that the long-run Phillips curve is steeper than the short-run Phillips curve. The only argument is whether it is vertical or not quite so vertical. And here the evidence is not quite all in. But there is a line of approach in analysis and reasoning which enables you to interpret, so far as I know, all the existing evidence consistently on the hypothesis of a long-run vertical Phillips curve.

3 THE COUNTER-REVOLUTION IN MONETARY THEORY[1]

Milton Friedman

Introduction

It is a great pleasure to be with you today, partly because I am honoured at being the first of the Harold Wincott lecturers,[2] partly because economics owes so much to the work that has been done on this island. Coming back to Britain, as I am fortunate enough to be able to do from time to time, always means coming back to a warm circle of friends or friendly enemies.

I am going to talk this afternoon primarily about a scientific development that has little ideological or political content. This development nonetheless has great relevance to governmental policy because it bears on the likely effects of particular kinds of governmental policy regardless of what party conducts the policy and for what purpose.

A counter-revolution must be preceded by two stages: an initial position from which there was a revolution, and the revolution. In order to set the stage, I would like first to make a few remarks about the initial position and the revolution.

It is convenient to have names to describe these positions. The

---

1   I chose this title because I used it about a dozen years ago for a talk at the London School of Economics. At that time, I was predicting. Now, I am reporting.

2   The first impression of this paper was the first Wincott Memorial Lecture in 1970.

initial position I shall call the quantity theory of money and associate it largely with the name of an American economist, Irving Fisher, although it is a doctrine to which many prominent English economists also made contributions. The revolution, as you all know, was made by Keynes in the 1930s. Keynes himself was a quantity theorist, so that his revolution was from, as it were, within the governing body. Keynes's name is the obvious name to attach to the revolution. The counter-revolution also needs a name, and perhaps the one most widely used in referring to it is 'the Chicago School'. More recently, however, it has been given a name which is less lovely but which has become so attached to it that I find it hard to avoid using it. That name is 'monetarism' because of the renewed emphasis on the role of the quantity of money.

A counter-revolution, whether in politics or in science, never restores the initial situation. It always produces a situation that has some similarity to the initial one but is also strongly influenced by the intervening revolution. That is certainly true of monetarism, which has benefited much from Keynes's work. Indeed I may say, as have so many others since there is no way of contradicting it, that if Keynes were alive today he would no doubt be at the forefront of the counter-revolution. You must never judge a master by his disciples.

Irving Fisher and the quantity theory

Let me then start briefly to set the stage with the initial position, the quantity theory of money as developed primarily by Irving Fisher, who is to my mind by far the greatest American economist. He was also an extraordinarily interesting and eccentric man. Indeed, I suspect that his professional reputation suffered during his life because he was not only an economist but also involved in many other activities, including being one of the leading members of the American prohibitionist party. He interviewed all potential presidential candidates for something like 30 years to find out what their position was on the subject of alcohol. His best-selling book, which has been translated into the largest number of languages, is not about economics at all but about health. It is about how to eat and keep healthy and is entitled *How to Live* (written jointly with Dr E. L. Fisk). But even that book is a tribute to his science. When he was a young man in his early thirties, he contracted tuberculosis, was given a year to live by his physicians, went out to the Far West where the air was good and proceeded to immerse himself in the study of health and methods of eating and so on. If we may judge the success of his scientific work by its results, he lived to the age of 80. As you may know, he was also a leading statistician, developed the theory of index numbers, worked in mathematics, economics and utility theory and had time enough besides to invent the Kardex filing system, the familiar system in which one little envelope flaps on another, so you can pull out a flat drawer to see what is in it. He founded what is now Remington-Rand Corporation in order to produce and distribute his invention. As you can see, he was a man of very wide interests and ability.

$MV = PT$

The basic idea of the quantity theory, that there is a relation between the quantity of money on the one hand and prices on the other, is surely one of the oldest ideas in economics. It goes back thousands of years. But it is one thing to express this idea in general terms. It is another thing to introduce system into the relation between money on the one hand and prices and other magnitudes on the other. What Irving Fisher did was to analyse the relationship in far greater detail than had ever been done earlier. He developed and popularised what has come to be known as the quantity equation: $MV = PT$, money multiplied by velocity equals prices multiplied by the volume of transactions. This is an equation that every college student of economics used to have to learn, then for a time did not, and now, as the counter-revolution has progressed, must again learn. Fisher not only presented this equation, he also applied it in a variety of contexts. He once wrote a famous article interpreting the business cycle as the 'dance of the dollar', in which he argued that fluctuations in economic activity were primarily a reflection of changes in the quantity of money. Perhaps even more pertinent to the present day, he analysed in detail the relation between inflation on the one hand and interest rates on the other. His first book on this subject, *Appreciation and Interest*, published in 1896, can be read today with profit and is immediately applicable to today's conditions.

In that work, Fisher made a distinction which again is something that went out of favour and has now come back into common use, namely the distinction between the nominal interest rate in pounds per year per hundred pounds and the real interest rate, i.e., corrected for the effect of changing prices. If you lend someone £100 today and in 12 months receive back £106, and if in the meantime prices rise by 6 per cent then your £106 will be worth no more than your £100 today. The nominal interest rate is 6 per cent, but the real interest rate is zero. This distinction between the nominal interest rate and the real interest rate is of the utmost importance in understanding the effects of monetary policy as well as the behaviour of interest rates. Fisher also distinguished sharply between the actual real rate, the rate realised after the event, and the anticipated real rate that lenders expected to receive or borrowers expected to pay. No one would lend money at 6 per cent if he expected prices to rise by 6 per cent during the year. If he did lend at 6 per cent, it must have been because he expected prices to rise by less than 6 per cent: the realised real rate was less than the anticipated real rate. This distinction between the actual real rate and the anticipated real rate is of the greatest importance today in understanding the course of events. It explains why inflation is so stubborn once it has become imbedded, because as inflation accelerates, people come to expect it. They come to build the expected inflation into the interest rates that they are willing to pay as borrowers or that they demand as lenders.

Wide consensus

Up to, let us say, the year 1930, Irving Fisher's analysis was widely accepted. In monetary theory, that analysis was taken to mean that in the quantity equation $MV = PT$ the term for velocity could be regarded as highly stable, that it could be taken as determined independently of the other terms in the equation, and that as a result changes in the quantity of money would be reflected either in prices or in output. It was also widely taken for granted that short-term fluctuations in the economy reflected changes in the quantity of money, or in the terms and conditions under which credit was available. It was taken for granted that the trend of prices over any considerable period reflected the behaviour of the quantity of money over that period.

In economic policy, it was widely accepted that monetary policy was the primary instrument available for stabilising the economy. Moreover, it was accepted that monetary policy should be operated largely through a combination of two blades of a scissors, the one blade being what we in the USA call 'discount rate' and you in Britain call 'Bank rate', the other blade being open-market operations, the purchase and sale of government securities.

That was more or less the initial doctrinal position prior to the Keynesian revolution. It was a position that was widely shared. Keynes's *A Tract on Monetary Reform*,[3] which I believe remains to this day one of his best books, reflects the consensus just described.

The Keynesian revolution

Then came the Keynesian revolution. What produced that revolution was the course of events. My colleague, George Stigler, in discussing the history of thought, has often argued that major changes within a discipline come from inside the discipline and are not produced by the impact of outside events. He may well be right in general. But in this particular instance I believe the basic source of the revolution and of the reaction against the quantity theory of money was a historical event, namely the great contraction or depression. In the United Kingdom, the contraction started in 1925 when Britain went back on gold at the pre-war parity and ended in 1931 when Britain went off gold. In the United States, the contraction started in 1929 and ended when the USA went off gold in early 1933. In both countries, economic conditions were depressed for years after the contraction itself had ended and an expansion had begun.

---

3   Macmillan, 1923.

Wrong lessons from the Great Depression

The Great Depression shattered the acceptance of the quantity theory of money because it was widely interpreted as demonstrating that monetary policy was ineffective, at least against a decline in business. All sorts of aphorisms were coined that are still with us, to indicate why it was that providing monetary ease would not necessarily lead to economic expansion, such as 'You can lead a horse to water but you can't make him drink' or 'Monetary policy is like a string: you can pull on it but you can't push on it', and doubtless there are many more.

As it happens, this interpretation of the depression was completely wrong. It turns out, as I shall point out more fully below, that on re-examination, the depression is a tragic testament to the effectiveness of monetary policy, not a demonstration of its impotence. But what mattered for the world of ideas was not what was true but what was believed to be true. And it was believed at the time that monetary policy had been tried and had been found wanting.

In part that view reflected the natural tendency for the monetary authorities to blame other forces for the terrible economic events that were occurring. The people who run monetary policy are human beings, even as you and I, and a common human characteristic is that if anything bad happens it is somebody else's fault. In the course of collaborating on a book on the monetary history of the United States, I had the dismal task of reading through 50 years of annual reports of the Federal Reserve Board. The only element that lightened that dreary task was the cyclical oscillation in the power attributed to monetary policy by the system. In good years the report would read 'Thanks to the excellent monetary policy of the Federal Reserve ...' In bad years the report would read 'Despite the excellent policy of the Federal Reserve ...', and it would go on to point out that monetary policy really was, after all, very weak and other forces so much stronger.

The monetary authorities proclaimed that they were pursuing easy money policies when in fact they were not, and their protestations were largely accepted. Hence Keynes, along with many others, concluded that monetary policy had been tried and found wanting. In contrast to most others, he offered an alternative analysis to explain why the depression had occurred and to indicate a way of ameliorating the situation.

Keynes's critique of the quantity theory

Keynes did not deny Irving Fisher's quantity equation. What Keynes said was something different. He said that, while of course MV equals PT, velocity, instead of being highly stable, is highly adaptable. If the quantity of money goes up, he said, what will happen is simply that the velocity of circulation of money will go down and nothing will happen on the other side of the equation to either prices or output. Correspondingly, if something pushes the right-hand side of the equation, PT or income, up without an increase in the quantity of money, all that will happen will be that velocity will rise. In other words, he said, velocity is a will-of-the-wisp. It can move one way or the other in response to changes either in the quantity of money or in income. The quantity of money is therefore of minor importance. (Since I am trying to cover highly technical material very briefly, I am leaving out many qualifications that are required for a full understanding of either Fisher or Keynes. I do want to stress that the statements I am making are simplifications and are not to be taken as a full exposition of any of the theories.)

What matters, said Keynes, is not the quantity of money. What matters is the part of total spending which is independent of current income, what has come to be called autonomous spending and to be identified in practice largely with investment by business and expenditures by government.

Keynes thereby directed attention away from the role of money and its relation to the flow of income and toward the relation between two flows of income, that which corresponds to autonomous spending and that which corresponds to induced spending. Moreover, he said, in the modern world, prices are highly rigid while quantities can change readily. When for whatever reason autonomous spending changes, the resulting change in income will manifest itself primarily in output and only secondarily and only after long lags in prices. Prices are determined by costs consisting mostly of wages, and wages are determined by the accident of past history.

The great contraction, he said, was the result of a collapse of demand for investment which in turn reflected a collapse of productive opportunities to use capital. Thus the engine and the motor of the great contraction was a collapse of investment transformed into a collapse of income by the multiplier process.

The implications for policy

This doctrine had far-reaching implications for economic policy. It meant that monetary policy was of little importance. Its only role was to keep interest rates down, both to reduce the pressure on the government budget in paying interest on its debts, and also because it might have a tiny bit of stimulating effect on investment. From this implication of the doctrine came the cheap money policy which was tried in country after country following World War II.

A second implication of the doctrine was that the major reliance for economic stabilisation could not be on monetary policy, as the quantity theorists had thought, but must be on fiscal policy, that is, on varying the rate of government spending and taxing.

A third implication was that inflation is largely to be interpreted as a cost-push phenomenon. It follows, although Keynes himself did not draw this conclusion from his doctrine, that the way to counteract inflation is through an incomes policy. If costs determine prices and costs are historically determined, then the way to stop any rise in prices is to stop the rise in costs.

These views became widely accepted by economists at large both as theory and as implications for policy. It is hard now at this distance in time to recognise how widely they were accepted. Let me just give you one quotation which could be multiplied manyfold, to give you the flavour of the views at the end of World War II. Parenthetically, acceptance of these views continued until more recently in Britain than in the United States, so it may be easier for you to recognise the picture I have been painting than it would be now for people in the United States. I quote from John H. Williams, who was a Professor of Economics at Harvard University, a principal adviser to the Federal Reserve Bank of New York, and widely regarded as an anti-Keynesian. In 1945 he wrote: 'I have long believed that the quantity of money by itself has a permissive rather than a positive effect on prices and production'. And in the sentence I want to stress he wrote: 'I can see no prospect of a revival of general monetary control in the post-war period'. That was a sweeping statement, and one that obviously proved very far indeed from the mark.

The high point in the United States of the application of Keynesian ideas to economic policy probably came with the new economists of the Kennedy administration. Their finest hour was the tax cut of 1964 which was premised entirely on the principles that I have been describing.

Having sketched briefly the initial stage of the quantity theory, and the revolutionary stage of the Keynesian theory, I come now to the monetarist counter-revolution.

The counter-revolution

As so often happens, just about the time that Keynes's ideas were being triumphant in practice, they were losing their hold on the minds of scholars in the academies. A number of factors contributed to a change of attitude towards the Keynesian doctrine. One was the experience immediately after World War II. On the basis of the Keynesian analysis, economists and others expected the war to be followed by another great depression. With our present experience of over two decades of inflation behind us it is hard to recognise that this was the sentiment of the times. But alike in the United States, in Great Britain and in many other countries, the dominant view was that, once World War II ended, once the pump-priming and government spending for military purposes ended, there would be an enormous economic collapse because of the scarcity of investment opportunities that had been given the blame for the Great Depression. Massive unemployment and massive deflation were the bugaboos of the time. As you all know, that did not happen. The problem after the war turned out to be inflation rather than deflation.

A second post-war experience that was important was the failure of cheap money policies. In Britain, Chancellor Dalton tried to follow the Keynesian policy of keeping interest rates very low. As you all know, he was unable to do so and had to give up. The same thing happened in the United States. The Federal Reserve System followed a policy of pegging bond prices, trying to keep interest rates down. It finally gave up in 1953 after the Treasury-Federal Reserve Accord of 1951 laid the groundwork for setting interest rates free. In country after country, wherever the cheap money policy was tried, it led to inflation and had to be abandoned. In no country was inflation contained until orthodox monetary policy was employed. Germany was one example in 1948; Italy shortly after; Britain and the United States later yet.

Reconsideration of the Great Depression

Another important element that contributed to a questioning of the Keynesian doctrine was a re-examination of monetary history and particularly of the Great Depression. When the evidence was examined in detail it turned out that bad monetary policy had to be given a very large share of the blame. In the United States, there was a reduction in the quantity of money by a third from 1929 to 1933. This reduction in the quantity of money clearly made the depression much longer and more severe than it otherwise would have been. Moreover, and equally important, it turned out that the reduction in the quantity of money was not a consequence of the unwillingness of horses to drink. It was not a consequence of being unable to push on a string. It was a direct consequence of the policies followed by the Federal Reserve system.

From 1930 to 1933, a series of bank runs and bank failures were permitted to run their course because the Federal Reserve failed to provide liquidity for the banking system, which was one of the main functions the designers of the Federal Reserve system intended it to perform. Banks failed because the public at large, fearful for the safety of their deposits, tried to convert their deposits into currency. In a fractional reserve system, it is literally impossible for all depositors to do that unless there is some source of additional currency. The Federal Reserve system was established in 1913 in response to the banking panic of 1907 primarily to provide additional liquidity at a time of pressure on banks. In 1930–33, the system failed to do so and it failed to do so despite the fact that there were many people in the system who were calling upon it to do so and who recognised that this was its correct function.

It was widely asserted at the time that the decline in the quantity of money was a consequence of the lack of willing borrowers. Perhaps the most decisive bit of evidence against that interpretation is that many banks failed because of a decline in the price of government securities. Indeed, it turned out that many banks that had made bad private loans came through much better than banks that had been cautious and had bought large amounts of Treasury and municipal securities for secondary liquidity. The reason was that there was a market for the government securities and hence when bank examiners came around to check on the banks, they had to mark down the price of the government's debt to the market value. However, there was no market for bad loans, and therefore they were carried on the books at face value. As a result, many careful, conservative banks failed.

The quantity of money fell by a third and roughly a third of all banks failed. This is itself a fascinating story and one that I can only touch on. The important point for our purposes is that it is crystal clear that at all times during the contraction, the Federal Reserve had it within its power to prevent the decline in the quantity of money and to produce an increase. Monetary policy had not been tried and found wanting. It had not been tried. Or, alternatively, it had been tried perversely. It had been used to force an incredible deflation on the American economy and on the rest of the world. If Keynes – and this is the main reason why I said what I did at the beginning – if Keynes had known the facts about the Great Depression as we now know them, he could not have interpreted that episode as he did.

Wider evidence

Another scholarly element that contributed to a reaction against the Keynesian doctrine and to the emergence of the new doctrine was extensive empirical analysis of the relation between the quantity of money on the one hand, and income, prices and interest rates on the other. Perhaps the simplest way for me to suggest why this was relevant is to recall that an essential element of the Keynesian doctrine was the passivity of velocity. If money rose, velocity would decline. Empirically, however, it turns out that the movements of velocity tend to reinforce those of money instead of to offset them. When the quantity of money declined by a third from 1929 to 1933 in the United States, velocity declined also. When the quantity of money rises rapidly in almost any country, velocity also rises rapidly. Far from velocity offsetting the movements of the quantity of money, it reinforces them.

I cannot go into the whole body of scientific work that has been done. I can only say that there has arisen an extensive literature concerned with exploring these relations which has demonstrated very clearly the existence of a consistent relation between changes in the quantity of money and changes in other economic magnitudes of a very different kind from that which Keynes assumed to exist.

The final blow, at least in the United States, to the Keynesian orthodoxy was a number of dramatic episodes in our recent domestic experience. These episodes centred around two key issues. The first was whether the behaviour of the quantity of money or rates of interest is a better criterion to use in conducting monetary policy. You have had a curious combination in this area of central bankers harking back to the real bills doctrine of the early 18th century on the one hand, and Keynesians on the other, who alike agreed that the behaviour of interest rates was the relevant criterion for the conduct of monetary policy. By contrast, the new interpretation is that interest rates are a misleading index of policy and that central bankers should look rather at the quantity of money. The second key issue was the relative role of fiscal policy and of monetary policy. By fiscal policy, I mean changes in government spending and taxing, holding the quantity of money constant. By monetary policy, I mean changes in the quantity of money, holding government spending and taxing constant.

Fiscal versus monetary policy

The problem in discussing the relative roles of fiscal policy and monetary policy is primarily to keep them separate, because in practice they operate jointly most of the time. Ordinarily if a government raises its spending without raising taxes, that is if it incurs a deficit in order to be expansionary, it will finance some of the deficit by printing money. Conversely if it runs a surplus, it will use part of that surplus to retire money. But from an analytical point of view, and from the point of view of getting at the issue that concerns the counter-revolution, it is important to consider fiscal policy and monetary policy separately, to consider each operating by itself. The Keynesians regarded as a clear implication of their position the proposition that fiscal policy by itself is important in affecting the level of income, that a large deficit would have essentially the same expansionary influence on the economy whether it was financed by borrowing from the public or by printing money.

The 'monetarists' rejected this proposition and maintained that fiscal policy by itself is largely ineffective, that what matters is what happens to the quantity of money. Off-hand that seems like an utterly silly idea. It seems absurd to say that if the government increases its expenditures without increasing taxes, that may not by itself be expansionary. Such a policy obviously puts income into the hands of the people to whom the government pays out its expenditures without taking any extra funds out of the hands of the taxpayers. Is that not obviously expansionary or inflationary? Up to that point, yes, but that is only half the story. We have to ask where the government gets the extra funds it spends. If the government prints money to meet its bills, that is monetary policy and we are trying to look at fiscal policy by itself. If the government gets the funds by borrowing from the public, then those people who lend the funds to the government have less to spend or to lend to others. The effect of the higher government expenditures may simply be higher spending by government and those who receive government funds and lower spending by those who lend to government or by those to whom lenders would have loaned the money instead. To discover any net effect on total spending, one must go to a more sophisticated level – to differences in the behaviour of the two groups of people or to effects of government borrowing on interest rates. There is no first-order effect.

Evidence from US 'experiments'

The critical first test on both these key issues came in the USA in 1966. There was fear of developing inflation and in the spring of 1966 the Federal Reserve Board, belatedly, stepped very hard on the brake. I say 'stepped very hard' because the record of the Federal Reserve over 50 years is that it has almost invariably acted too much too late. Almost always it has waited too long before acting and then acted too strongly. In 1966, the result was a combination of a very tight monetary policy, under which the quantity of money did not grow at all during the final nine months of the year, and a very expansive fiscal policy. So you had a nice experiment. Which was going to dominate? The tight money policy or the easy fiscal policy? The Keynesians in general argued that the easy fiscal policy was going to dominate and therefore predicted continued rapid expansion in 1967. The monetarists argued that monetary policy would dominate, and so it turned out. There was a definite slowing down in the rate of growth of economic activity in the first half of 1967, following the tight money policy of 1966. When, in early 1967, the Federal Reserve reversed its policy and started to print money like mad, about six or nine months later, after the usual lag, income recovered and a rapid expansion in economic activity followed. Quite clearly, monetary policy had dominated fiscal policy in that encounter.

A still more dramatic example came in 1968 and from 1968 to 1970. In the summer of 1968, under the influence of the Council of Economic Advisers and at the recommendation of President Johnson, Congress enacted a surtax of 10 per cent on income. It was enacted in order to fight the inflation which was then accelerating. The believers in the Keynesian view were so persuaded of the potency of this weapon that they were afraid of 'overkill'. They thought the tax increase might be too much and might stop the economy in its tracks. They persuaded the Federal Reserve system, or I should rather say that the Federal Reserve system was of the same view. Unfortunately for the United States, but fortunately for scientific knowledge, the Federal Reserve accordingly decided that it had best offset the overkill effects of fiscal policy by expanding the quantity of money rapidly. Once again, we had a beautiful controlled experiment with fiscal policy extremely tight and monetary policy extremely easy. Once again, there was a contrast between two sets of predictions. The Keynesians or fiscalists argued that the surtax would produce a sharp slow-down in the first half of 1969 at the latest while the monetarists argued that the rapid growth in the quantity of money would more than offset the fiscal effects, so that there would be a continued inflationary boom in the first half of 1969. Again, the monetarists proved correct. Then, in December 1968, the Federal Reserve Board did move to tighten money in the sense of slowing down the rate of growth of the quantity of money and that was followed after the appropriate interval by a slow-down in the economy. This test, I may say, is still in process at the time of this lecture, but up to now it again seems to be confirming the greater importance of the monetary than of the fiscal effect.

'This is where I came in'

One swallow does not make a spring. My own belief in the greater importance of monetary policy does not rest on these dramatic episodes. It rests on the experience of hundreds of years and of many countries. These episodes of the past few years illustrate that effect; they do not demonstrate it. Nonetheless, the public at large cannot be expected to follow the great masses of statistics. One dramatic episode is far more potent in influencing public opinion than a pile of well-digested, but less dramatic, episodes. The result in the USA at any rate has been a drastic shift in opinion, both professional and lay.

This shift, so far as I can detect, has been greater in the United States than in the United Kingdom. As a result, I have had in the UK the sensation that I am sure all of you have had in a continuous cinema when you come to the point where you say, 'Oh, this is where I came in.' The debate about monetary effects in Britain is pursuing the identical course that it pursued in the United States about five or so years ago. I am sure that the same thing must have happened in the 1930s. When the British economists wandered over to the farther shores among their less cultivated American brethren, bringing to them the message of Keynes, they must have felt, as I have felt coming to these shores in the opposite direction, that this was where they came in. I am sure they then encountered the same objections that they had encountered in Britain five years earlier. And so it is today. Criticism of the monetary doctrines in this country today is at the naive, unsophisticated level we encountered in the USA about five or more years ago.

Thanks to the very able and active group of economists in this country who are currently working on the monetary statistics, and perhaps even more to the effect which the course of events will have, I suspect that the developments in this country will continue to imitate those in the United States. Not only in this area, but in other areas as well, I have had the experience of initially being in a small minority and have had the opportunity to observe the scenario that unfolds as an idea gains wider acceptance. There is a standard pattern. When anybody threatens an orthodox position, the first reaction is to ignore the interloper. The less said about him the better. But if he begins to win a hearing and gets annoying, the second reaction is to ridicule him, make fun of him as an extremist, a foolish fellow who has these silly ideas. After that stage passes the next, and the most important, stage is to put on his clothes. You adopt for your own his views, and then attribute to him a caricature of those views saying, 'He's an extremist, one of those fellows who says only money matters – everybody knows that sort. Of course money does matter, but ...'

Key propositions of monetarism

Let me finally describe the state to which the counter-revolution has come by listing systematically the central propositions of monetarism.

1. There is a consistent though not precise relation between the rate of growth of the quantity of money and the rate of growth of nominal income. (By nominal income, I mean income measured in pounds sterling or in dollars or in francs, not real income, income measured in real goods.) That is, whether the amount of money in existence is growing by 3 per cent a year, 5 per cent a year or 10 per cent a year will have a significant effect on how fast nominal income grows. If the quantity of money grows rapidly, so will nominal income; and conversely.

2. This relation is not obvious to the naked eye largely because it takes time for changes in monetary growth to affect income and how long it takes is itself variable. The rate of monetary growth today is not very closely related to the rate of income growth

today. Today's income growth depends on what has been happening to money in the past. What happens to money today affects what is going to happen to income in the future.

3. On the average, a change in the rate of monetary growth produces a change in the rate of growth of nominal income about six to nine months later. This is an average that does not hold in every individual case. Sometimes the delay is longer, sometimes shorter. But I have been astounded at how regularly an average delay of six to nine months is found under widely different conditions. I have studied the data for Japan, for India, for Israel, for the United States. Some of our students have studied it for Canada and for a number of South American countries. Whichever country you take, you generally get a delay of around six to nine months. How clear-cut the evidence for the delay is depends on how much variation there is in the quantity of money. The Japanese data have been particularly valuable because the Bank of Japan was very obliging for some 15 years from 1948 to 1963 and produced very wide movements in the rate of change in the quantity of money. As a result, there is no ambiguity in dating when it reached the top and when it reached the bottom. Unfortunately for science, in 1963 they discovered monetarism and they started to increase the quantity of money at a fairly stable rate and now we are not able to get much more information from the Japanese experience.

4. The changed rate of growth of nominal income typically shows up first in output and hardly at all in prices. If the rate of monetary growth is reduced then about six to nine months later, the rate of growth of nominal income and also of physical output will decline. However, the rate of price rise will be affected very little. There will

be downward pressure on prices only as a gap emerges between actual and potential output.

5. On the average, the effect on prices comes about six to nine months after the effect on income and output, so the total delay between a change in monetary growth and a change in the rate of inflation averages something like 12–18 months. That is why it is a long road to hoe to stop an inflation that has been allowed to start. It cannot be stopped overnight.

6. Even after allowance for the delay in the effect of monetary growth, the relation is far from perfect. There's many a slip 'twixt the monetary change and the income change.

7. In the short run, which may be as much as five or ten years, monetary changes affect primarily output. Over decades, on the other hand, the rate of monetary growth affects primarily prices. What happens to output depends on real factors: the enterprise, ingenuity and industry of the people; the extent of thrift; the structure of industry and government; the relations among nations, and so on.

8. It follows from the propositions I have so far stated that *inflation is always and everywhere a monetary phenomenon* in the sense that it is and can be produced only by a more rapid increase in the quantity of money than in output. However, there are many different possible reasons for monetary growth, including gold discoveries, financing of government spending, and financing of private spending.

9. Government spending may or may not be inflationary. It clearly will be inflationary if it is financed by creating money, that is, by printing currency or creating bank deposits. If it is financed by taxes or by borrowing from the public, the main effect is that the government spends the funds instead of the taxpayer or instead of the lender or instead of the person who would otherwise have borrowed the funds. Fiscal policy is extremely important in determining what fraction of total national income is spent by government and who bears the burden of that expenditure. By itself, it is not important for inflation. (This is the proposition about fiscal and monetary policy that I discussed earlier.)

10. One of the most difficult things to explain in simple fashion is the way in which a change in the quantity of money affects income. Generally, the initial effect is not on income at all, but on the prices of existing assets, bonds, equities, houses, and other physical capital. This effect, the liquidity effect stressed by Keynes, is an effect on the balance-sheet, not on the income account. An increased rate of monetary growth, whether produced through open-market operations or in other ways, raises the amount of cash that people and businesses have relative to other assets. The holders of the now excess cash will try to adjust their portfolios by buying other assets. But one man's spending is another man's receipts. All the people together cannot change the amount of cash all hold – only the monetary authorities can do that. However, as people *attempt* to change their cash balances, the effect spreads from one asset to another. This tends to raise the prices of assets and to reduce interest rates, which encourages spending to produce new assets and also encourages spending on current services rather than on purchasing existing assets. That is how the initial effect on

balance-sheets gets translated into an effect on income and spending. The difference in this area between the monetarists and the Keynesians is not on the nature of the process, but on the range of assets considered. The Keynesians tend to concentrate on a narrow range of marketable assets and recorded interest rates. The monetarists insist that a far wider range of assets and of interest rates must be taken into account. They give importance to such assets as durable and even semi-durable consumer goods, structures and other real property. As a result, they regard the market interest rates stressed by the Keynesians as only a small part of the total spectrum of rates that are relevant.

11. One important feature of this mechanism is that a change in monetary growth affects interest rates in one direction at first but in the opposite direction later on. More rapid monetary growth at first tends to lower interest rates. But later on, as it raises spending and stimulates price inflation, it also produces a rise in the demand for loans which will tend to raise interest rates. In addition, rising prices introduce a discrepancy between real and nominal interest rates. That is why world-wide interest rates are highest in the countries that have had the most rapid rise in the quantity of money and also in prices – countries like Brazil, Chile or Korea. In the opposite direction, a slower rate of monetary growth at first raises interest rates but later on, as it reduces spending and price inflation, lowers interest rates. That is why world-wide interest rates are lowest in countries that *have had* the slowest rate of growth in the quantity of money – countries like Switzerland and Germany.

This two-edged relation between money and interest rates explains why monetarists insist that interest rates are a highly misleading guide to monetary policy. This is one respect in which the monetarist doctrines have already had a significant effect on US policy. The Federal Reserve in January 1970 shifted from primary reliance on 'money market conditions' (i.e., interest rates) as a criterion of policy to primary reliance on 'monetary aggregates' (i.e., the quantity of money).

The relations between money and yields on assets (interest rates and stock market earnings-price ratios) are even lower than between money and nominal income. Apparently, factors other than monetary growth play an extremely important part. Needless to say, we do not know in detail what they are, but that they are important we know from the many movements in interest rates and stock market prices which cannot readily be connected with movements in the quantity of money.

Concluding cautions

These propositions clearly imply both that monetary policy is important and that the important feature of monetary policy is its effect on the quantity of money rather than on bank credit or total credit or interest rates. They also imply that wide swings in the rate of change of the quantity of money are destabilising and should be avoided. But beyond this, differing implications are drawn.

Some monetarists conclude that deliberate changes in the rate of monetary growth by the authorities can be useful to offset other forces making for instability, provided they are gradual and take into account the lags involved. They favour fine tuning, using changes in the quantity of money as the instrument of policy. Other monetarists, including myself, conclude that our present understanding of the relation between money, prices and output is so meagre, that there is so much leeway in these relations, that such discretionary changes do more harm than good. We believe that an automatic policy under which the quantity of money would grow at a steady rate – month-in, month-out, year-in, year-out – would provide a stable monetary framework for economic growth without itself being a source of instability and disturbance.

One of the most widespread misunderstandings of the monetarist position is the belief that this prescription of a stable rate of growth in the quantity of money derives from our confidence in a rigid connection between monetary change and economic change. The situation is quite the opposite. If I really believed in a precise, rigid, mechanical connection between money and income, if also I thought that I knew what it was and if I thought that the central bank shared that knowledge with me, which is an even larger 'if', I would then say that we should use the knowledge to offset other forces making for instability. However, I do not believe any of these 'ifs' to be true. On the average, there is a close relation between changes in the quantity of money and the subsequent course of national income. But economic policy must deal with the individual case, not the average. In any one case, there is much slippage. It is precisely this leeway, this looseness in the relation, this lack of a mechanical one-to-one correspondence between changes in money and in income that is the primary reason why I have long favoured for the USA a quasi-automatic monetary policy under which the quantity of money would grow at a steady rate of 4 or 5 per cent per year, month-in, month-out. (The desirable rate of growth will differ from country to country depending on the trends in output and money-holding propensities.)

There is a great deal of evidence from the past of attempts by monetary authorities to do better. The verdict is very clear. The attempts by monetary authorities to do better have done far more harm than good. The actions by the monetary authorities have been an important source of instability. As I have already indicated, the actions of the US monetary authorities were responsible for the 1929–33 catastrophe. They were responsible equally for the recent acceleration of inflation in the USA. That is why I have been and remain strongly opposed to discretionary monetary policy – at least until such time as we demonstrably know enough to limit discretion by more sophisticated rules than the steady-rate-of-growth rule I have suggested. That is why I have come to stress the danger of assigning too much weight to monetary policy. Just as I believe that Keynes's disciples went further than he himself would have gone, so I think there is a danger that people who find that a few good predictions have been made by using monetary aggregates will try to carry that relationship further than it can go. Three years ago I wrote:

> We are in danger of assigning to monetary policy a
> larger role than it can perform, in danger of asking it to
> accomplish tasks that it cannot achieve and, as a result, in
> danger of preventing it from making the contribution that it
> is capable of making.[4]

A steady rate of monetary growth at a moderate level can provide a framework under which a country can have little inflation and much growth. It will not produce perfect stability; it will not produce heaven on earth; but it can make an important contribution to a stable economic society.

---

4   Milton Friedman, 'The Role of Monetary Policy', Presidential Address to the American Economic Association, 29 December 1967: *American Economic Review*, March 1968 (reprinted in *The Optimum Quantity of Money and Other Essays*, Aldine Publishing, 1969, pp. 95–110 – quotation from p. 99).

4 THE CONSTITUTIONAL POSITION OF THE CENTRAL BANK

Charles A. E. Goodhart

THE THIRTY-SECOND WINCOTT LECTURE

8 OCTOBER 2002

Introduction

The *Financial Times* has been blessed over the last half-century with a series of writers whose weekly columns are eagerly awaited. When I first started reading the *FT*, at the end of the 1950s, Harold Wincott's regular Wednesday column was the first item to which I turned, to be followed by such as Sir Samuel Brittan and Martin Wolf. This continuing line of great columnists has edified and instructed those interested in the British and world economy now for decades.

I feel confident that Harold Wincott would have approved of granting operational independence to central banks, in part since it constrains the ability of the government to intervene in financial markets for purely political reasons. Moreover, he could have explained this all in lucid English, in the imaginary dialogues between himself and his son, and later his grandson, without the use of academically fashionable jargon, such as 'time inconsistency'.

Independence for central banks

In the course of the almost worldwide move towards granting central banks operational independence, there have been several interrelated strands of argument. The first arose as a reaction in New Zealand to Prime Minister Muldoon's interference with, and political manipulation of, every aspect of that country's economy, but particularly of its public sector, during the 1980s, an episode which illustrates that government interference in the economy can emanate from right-wing governments as much as from those on the left. The question which the then in-coming Labour government, and its finance minister, Roger Douglas, sought to answer was how to minimise constant political interference in the public sector and yet at the same time achieve commonly agreed objectives in the provision of public services; in the case of monetary policy that service being primarily price stability. If such objectives could be obtained through competition and the pursuit of profit maximisation, then the correct policy response was, of course, privatisation. In other cases, the general answer that was found was to specify, as closely as possible, the objectives to be attained by the public sector bodies responsible for achieving them, in a contract with the government, and then to leave the managers with the freedom to make the necessary operational decisions, subject to strict accountability for the achievement of *outcomes* (though not for processes or methods, as those of us in universities who have suffered from the appalling Quality Assurance Authority studies on teaching methods would wish to emphasise). In this context operational independence for the Reserve Bank of New Zealand (RBNZ) was not primarily about the specifics of monetary policy, but rather the application to the RBNZ of a generalised approach to public sector bodies, which had already been applied to numerous other New Zealand public sector industries and services.

The second strand of argument relates to the danger that an executive, and the legislature, having together established the underlying laws and regulations by which a country should be run, might then be tempted to bend or to subvert the subsequent legal and operational rulings in their own short-run political interest. This danger is all the greater because the executive, especially when it dominates the legislature, as it is designed to do here in the UK, has great power. It is this concern which leads to the separation of the judiciary, the least dangerous of the three main arms of government, from the executive and legislature, so that the interpretation and enforcement of the rules of law are carried out through an independent judiciary, though here, as elsewhere, accountability and transparency are essential to maintain democratic legitimacy. The people have a right to know the legal grounds on which a case has been settled.

Within the field of monetary policy, the potential subversion of the underlying objective of price stability goes under the jargon terminology of 'time inconsistency', which harks back to the famous Kydland and Prescott paper (1977). That demonstrated how long-term commitments would often be forgone in pursuit of short-term (electoral) expediency. Much of that literature, following certain strands of American thought, exaggerates political venality, suggesting for example that politicians consciously try to fool the public by covertly expanding monetary growth prior to elections. Considering that the monetary policy instrument involves setting interest rates, which is a highly visible process, and that the effects of this on the economy require long and variable lags, the implausibility of instigating a covert political business cycle via monetary manipulations is clear. The same holds true, more or less, when the policy instrument is some form of monetary base, or monetary aggregate, control, the data for which are usually rapidly available.

Nevertheless, there are milder forms of time inconsistency. Because of those very same lags, interest rate increases now need to be made to counter forecast inflation threats in the future, say 18 to 24 months hence. But forecasts of the likely onset of inflation at such a future date are inherently uncertain, and increases in interest rates, which thereby also tend to depress asset prices, are widely unpopular. Hence politicians are loath to raise interest rates just on the basis of forecasts, but would rather wait until there is clear and present evidence of rising inflation. But by then it is too late to nip the inflationary pressure in the bud. The shortcomings of policy, in this country at least, have been 'too little, too late', not a conscious attempt to rig elections. Indeed, we have recently seen, even within our own independent Monetary Policy Committee (MPC), the tensions that can occur when a forecast of rising future inflation coincides with current low present values of that same variable.

These two arguments for operational independence were in turn greatly strengthened by the claim, nowadays widely if not quite universally accepted, that demand management cannot on its own enhance either the medium- and longer-term growth rate, or the sustainable level of employment, beyond the limits enforced by more fundamental supply-side considerations; or in other words that the long-term Phillips curve, relating inflation to the output gap, was vertical. This is not to deny, however, that badly judged demand-side management can depress the economy below potentially attainable levels for very long periods, as Argentina over many decades and Japan more recently have evidenced.

But if the medium- and longer-term Phillips curve is vertical, then over this same horizon the only objective that the central bank *can* achieve is price stability. Indeed, for a variety of reasons such price stability will also provide the best nominal background for growth; though it is arguable that price stability is better treated in practice as involving a small positive rate of inflation, rather than zero inflation or perhaps even deflation.

The key result of this line of analysis is that a central bank should have a single, measurable and quantifiable primary policy objective, to wit the rate of inflation. Hence accountability and visibility are enhanced. There are no trade-offs; no discretionary judgements between competing objectives. Moreover, when the government is involved in establishing the objective, by defining the proposed path for the inflation target, there is no democratic deficit either. Indeed, the public accountability of monetary policy has been greater in this country since 1997, when the in-coming Labour government changed the regime, than in any previous period.

Milton Friedman (1962) dissented from this policy proposal in his paper 'Should there be an Independent Monetary Authority?' on the grounds that

> the objectives [of price stability that] it specifies are
> ones that the monetary authorities do not have the
> clear and direct power to achieve by their own actions.
> It consequently raises the earlier problem of dispersing
> responsibilities and leaving the authorities too much
> leeway. There is unquestionably a close connection between
> monetary actions and the price level. But the connection is
> not so close, so invariable, or so direct that the objective of
> achieving a stable price level is an appropriate guide to the
> day-to-day activities of the authorities.

I disagree. Most outcomes in life are not under the complete control of the relevant decision-maker, for example promotion for football managers, financial returns for fund managers, profits for company CEOs, growth for economic ministries. Yet they are judged, and rightly so, by such outcomes.

Independent fiscal authorities?

Delegation of decision-making is, however, far more difficult when trade-offs among competing objectives are involved. It is possible to argue that the role of politics is to try to resolve and reconcile instances in which there *are* such inherent trade-offs. For example, so great has been the success of delegating monetary policy to an independent central bank that many ask why the same trick cannot be turned with fiscal policy. Thus Alan Blinder (1998), in his Robbins lectures on *Central Banking in Theory and Practice*, commented that:

> having briefly presented the basic arguments for central bank independence, let me now raise a curmudgeonly thought. When you think deeply about the reasons for removing monetary policy decisions from the 'political thicket', you realise that the reasons apply just as well to many other aspects of economic policy – and, indeed, to non-economic policy as well. Consider tax policy as an example.
>
> Decisions on the structure of the tax code clearly require a long time horizon, just as monetary policy decisions do, because their allocative and distributional effects will reverberate for years to come. There is a constant temptation – which needs to be resisted – to reach for short-term gain that can have negative long-run consequences. Capital levies are a particularly clear example. Tax design and incidence theory are complex matters, requiring considerable technical expertise, just as monetary policy

is. And decisions on tax policy are probably even more susceptible to interest-group politics than decisions on monetary policy.

Yet, while many democratic societies have independent central banks, every one leaves tax policy in the hands of elected politicians. In fact, no one even talks about turning over tax policy to an independent agency. Why? I leave this question as food for thought, perhaps for another day [from Chapter 3 on Central Bank Independence, pp. 56–9].

One answer to this conundrum is that, unlike monetary policy which has the one single overriding objective of maintaining price stability, fiscal policy is intrinsically concerned with at least three objectives, these being allocative efficiency, income distribution and macroeconomic stabilisation and adjustment. Any fiscal package will tend to affect each of these in different ways, so trade-offs are almost inevitable, and the resolution of such trade-offs would seem to require a political decision-making process.

There have, however, been occasional attempts to reduce the dimension of such political horse-trading in the fiscal arena by seeking to separate decisions on the overall macroeconomic magnitudes – for example, to force a decision on the aggregate size of the fiscal deficit, separate from subsequent, second-round decisions on the individual elements of the budget. This is particularly common, and indeed necessary, when several states with independent fiscal powers share a single, federal monetary system. Otherwise spill-overs from the individual states' fiscal decisions into the common monetary system could all too easily lead to an untenable tension between the fiscal policies of the separate states and the single federal monetary policy, and, in particular, to concern about whether a federal government might be induced to bail out a bankrupt subsidiary state. While the possibility of such a bail-out would surely be denied in advance, there would be enormous pressure to do so after the event, a clear case of likely 'time inconsistency'. Hence the constitutional requirement in most states in the USA for a balanced budget; the Amsterdam Stability and Growth Pact; and the serious problems which have been evident recently in Argentina and previously in Brazil, until they resolved this matter.

Nevertheless, in most such federal cases, for example in the USA, externally imposed limits on the fiscal deficit of the subsidiary states have been accompanied by a discretionary and politically determined federal budget deficit, which is typically much larger than the subsidiary state budgets. The euro-zone is an exception in this respect. Even so, as Geoffrey Wood has reminded me, the checks and balances in the budgetary process in the USA at least, and the long time lags involved, have meant that the quasi-automatic fiscal stabilisers have usually played a more successful role in stabilisation than conscious discretionary policy.

This does raise the question of whether, besides the appropriate limitation on *subsidiary* state budgets, there should be independent decisions, or outside constraints, on the *aggregate* budget deficit either of unitary, or of federal, countries. There are many considerations. For example, the macroeconomic effect of a given overall deficit is not independent of the composition of its component items. Again, how should one respond to the working of the automatic stabilisers in influencing the deficit? Next, given the penchant of politicians for believing that a cyclical upturn is due to their own genius in generating a better trend so that no need is then seen for achieving a surplus during the good times, a non-cyclically adjusted constraint is likely to lead to the stabilisers being switched off just when they are most needed. However, the measurement of such cyclical adjustment factors is an arcane mystery, and accounting practices in the public sector have been every bit as creative as those alleged to have been used in the private sector in certain companies.

One final point that I would raise is to query what the objective for a (putatively independently determined) aggregate fiscal deficit would be, so that *ex post* accountability could be applied. It cannot be the level of employment, because the vertical Phillips curve analysis indicates that this is the province of underlying supply-side factors. It cannot be price stability because that is the task of monetary policy. Presumably, then, the function of aggregate fiscal policy is to help to determine the balance between public and private sector expenditures, between expenditure on tradable products and that on non-tradables, and thus the level of exchange rates and (real) interest rates consistent with price stability. So, if public sector expenditures, and the overall deficit, are bigger, real interest rates then have to be higher, with a higher real exchange rate, in order to maintain the mandated level of price stability. But that would seem to bring us right back to issues of allocative efficiency and of income distribution. If so, the idea that we could seek to avoid trade-offs and conflicts between objectives, by separating off decisions about the aggregate fiscal deficit from detailed assessment of its component parts, would seem to be a mirage.

Competing objectives in monetary policy

One of the arguments pressed most strongly by the Treasury in this country *against* operational independence had been that the various arms of demand management, notably, but not only, fiscal and monetary policies, needed to be coordinated, and could not be so if monetary policy was delegated to the central bank. While this appears superficially sensible, in practice one arm of policy has always been first mover, aiming at internal stability, whereas the other arm has had more responsibility for the exchange rate and the composition of expenditures between tradables and non-tradables. In previous decades fiscal policy was first mover and monetary policy had the compositional role. Now the responsibilities have just been reversed, but coordination remains no more difficult or problematical than it ever was.

A corollary of this analysis is that, once the central bank has been given the target of achieving price stability, the onus for influencing the level of exchange rates and interest rates effectively falls on fiscal policy. This is not widely recognised, but leads to some uncomfortable questions. How far would the public have wanted to enjoy lower exchange rates and interest rates in recent years if the quid pro quo for doing so was lower public expenditures or higher taxes? This is the way that most central bankers think that this key economic trade-off *should* be discussed, but it does not yet appear in this format to the man in the street. One question that should be asked is why this relationship, so clear in the view of central bankers, has not been more widely appreciated by the general public.

So, under a system of inflation targets, the internal/external balance is essentially an issue for fiscal policy to address. But that does not mean that monetary policy can be totally innocent of trade-offs, despite its one objective, one instrument format. In particular, there is a *short-run* trade-off between inflation and output; over that horizon the Phillips curve is downward sloping, though the precise position of this relationship remains subject to unpredictable and elusive variation. Indeed, one of the main routes by which the central bank aims to achieve its medium-run inflation target is by trying to adjust current real output relative to its (imprecisely) estimated equilibrium level; and by the same token nominal interest rates changes have real effects on expenditures and output in the short run.

Does that not get one back into the realm of value judgements over trade-offs between alternative objectives? Not really, in the UK case at least. The point here is that the clash between output and inflation objectives only really arises when there are supply shocks. With a demand shock, the adjustment required to stabilise inflation will at the same time bring output back into line with equilibrium, *ceteris paribus*. It is supply shocks which cause the difficulty, driving inflation and output in different directions away from their desired levels. But any *major* adverse supply shock, especially if unexpected, such as a conflict-driven oil price increase, or destruction of output capacity, is likely to drive inflation outside the 1 per cent band around the target which triggers a public letter from the MPC to the Chancellor. In that letter the MPC is expected not only to explain what has happened, but also to present its plans for returning inflation to target, which will involve, at least implicitly, a forecast path for output as well as for inflation – in other words, how the MPC intends to address that trade-off.

What has not been widely enough appreciated is that this letter gives the Chancellor an opportunity to write back; there could be an *exchange* of letters. If the Chancellor dislikes how the MPC plans to handle the trade-off in this circumstance, he can always respond by asking, for example, the Bank to accelerate the return to the inflation target, thereby raising the coefficient and weighting placed on reducing the variability of inflation, around target, relative to that on output. Or alternatively he can do the opposite, asking the Bank to give more weight to output smoothing, rather than inflation smoothing, in that conjuncture. So, very cleverly, the current regime of inflation targeting in the UK has an inbuilt mechanism for restoring the decision-making process to the political arena whenever the short-term trade-offs look to become really difficult and potentially contentious.

There are those who query whether such safety-valve, or override, mechanisms may not do more harm than good, notably by reducing the economic credibility of a central bank's independence. Chris Huhne has made this point in the *Financial Times*, in a personal opinion piece on 20 June 2002. But central bank independence is essentially a political construct, so that if too large a head of steam develops on the political front, then that independence could get blown away. Credibility has a most important political dimension. Of course, a central bank's independence can be further protected, and shored up, against political involvement by being incorporated in a constitution or a binding treaty; and that does mean that safety valves, and overrides, may be seen as less necessary. Even so, I rather doubt that it would be either intrinsically desirable, or sensible in its own self-interest, for a central bank to flout too far and for too long the democratically expressed value judgements of the people, and of their representatives in government, about the balance between competing objectives.

The central bank and financial stability

Central banking is not just about maintaining an anchor for price stability; it has historically also had a vital concern for the stability of the financial system as a whole, and particularly for the banking and payments systems within that. The achievement of systemic financial stability is a much more complex issue than that of trying to hit an inflation target. The measurement of financial stability is conceptually much more difficult; there is no single obvious instrument to adjust, if unilateral adjustment can be made expeditiously at all; and in the case of financial stability one is concerned about extreme, and hence improbable, events rather than central tendencies. For all such reasons accountability, except in a rather trivial *ex post* sense, is much more difficult. I intend to write more about such issues over the next few years.

What I want to do now is to note that commercial banks, and banking, are more intimately connected with assets, and asset prices, than with the course of goods and services prices more widely. Bank lending is primarily for asset purchases, and when it is collateralised, the collateral involves assets, not goods and services. In this context domestic real estate, housing and property, has been and remains much more important than either equities, or foreign assets, in the nexus between banking and asset prices. If one worries about systemic stability in banking, one should worry most about property prices rather than the FTSE or the Dow Jones indices.

That raises the question of whether there can be a trade-off between maintaining stability in asset prices, in particular property prices, and hence also in systemic stability in the financial system on the one hand, and in controlling retail price inflation or goods and services inflation on the other. Some of the practical problems of trying to take account of asset prices are well illustrated by the contrasting trends in housing and equity prices in the UK so far in

2002. More generally, however, there is usually *little* conflict between the policy needs indicated by asset prices, and for systemic stability, on the one hand, and the needs indicated by goods and services prices, and for price stability, on the other. Long periods of asset price deflation, and financial fragility, typically go hand in hand with falling or sluggish output and deflation – witness Japan now and the US in the 1930s. Similarly booming asset prices usually occur on the back of strongly growing economies and inflationary upsurges. But there are exceptions. The stock market crash in 1972–4 in London was *far* worse than anything seen recently, and this occurred at a time of sharply worsening inflation. In the last decade the very success of monetary policy in lowering inflation, inflationary expectations and hence nominal interest rates, and also in presiding over one of the longest cyclical economic upturns ever, played some part in encouraging the boom in asset prices, especially of equities.

If we had anticipated market movements in 2001 and 2002, would we have wanted to raise interest rates a bit more and a bit earlier in 1999 and 2000, perhaps especially in the USA? In my view the answer to this is 'yes', though even so I doubt that with perfect hindsight the interest rate path would have been much higher then. The point of this counter-factual is to contend that the main problem in trying to take asset prices into account in setting monetary policy is not so much the principle of whether it is desirable to do so, but rather the difficulty of assessing the extent of any current disequilibrium and of forecasting the future path of such prices over the policy horizon.

Alan Greenspan's famous comment about irrational exuberance occurred in 1996 when the Dow Jones Index was still between 6000 and 7000. It is arguable that, if you make the appropriate adjustments for inflation, real interest rates, dividend payments, etc., values have finally fallen back in 2002 to less exuberant levels. But it took six years. Would he, even with perfect hindsight, have been right to raise interest rates before, say, 1999? The argument that the authorities can stabilise output and inflation by preventing a boom/bust bubble cycle in asset prices depends on their ability to forecast that asset price cycle. This is not an easy exercise. After all, in the short and even the medium term, asset prices tend in most cases (though not in real estate) to follow a random path. Only in the long run, of five to ten years or more, is there mean reversion; and monetary policy, and inflation control, have a horizon of a year or two, not of decades.

At this point some of my European Central Bank friends and colleagues might surmise that their first pillar for assessing policy, watching the appropriate trends in broad money, might protect against longer-term monetary policy errors, especially given the close links between asset prices and bank lending developments. While I do believe that monetary variables often contain useful information, rather an unfashionable position nowadays in Anglo-Saxon central banks, the ongoing structural shifts in banking, which are also affected by regulatory changes, sometimes make it extremely difficult to decipher the message in the monetary data.

So where does that leave me on the broad question of whether it is right to take asset price developments, and the associated effect on financial stability, into account in trying to set monetary policy? My own answer to this is that it is correct to do so in principle, but that the practical problems of forecasting the current disequilibrium and future time path of asset prices are so severe that one is talking at most about shading monetary policy decisions on this account; and this, I guess, is what tends to happen already, though probably more often in response to asset price declines than to increases, for rather obvious reasons.

Structure of the central bank

Let me end with a few thoughts about the relationship between central bank independence and the putative problem of a democratic deficit. These are based on the counter-factual thought experiment, suggested to me by my colleague Professor Geoffrey Miller at New York University, of the possibility of individuals presenting themselves for a contested democratic *election* to positions in the MPC, or even to be governor of the central bank. After all, quite a sizeable proportion of the US judiciary, at the state level, are elected, not appointed, and that is an independent arm of government. If you can elect attorney generals and local judges, why not members of the MPC?

Let us start with the case of an independent central bank that has a modicum of goal independence; that is to say, its remit allows it some room to choose between alternative policy objectives, to make value judgements between trade-offs. In that case a democratic election for central bankers would give them greater legitimacy to maintain and support their own preferences and value judgements relative to that of the separately elected government. But that would exacerbate conflict, and harm coordination, between the two separate centres of economic policy and control. As was noted earlier, in a system in which the single objective of the MPC is mandated by the central government, there is neither a democratic deficit nor any real coordination problems. In a world where the MPC could juggle several objectives, and also received a separate mandate from the electorate through direct elections, that would be a recipe for rivalry between power centres and coordination failure. It is difficult to see how any such discordant system could last for long.

Let us shift from the example where the central bank has some partial goal independence to the more normal, and in my view more appropriate, case where it has operational independence only. In this instance the central bank has no, or very limited, scope for value judgements; its job is to achieve a pre-selected target. That requires, above all, technical professional ability, and not a set of preferences over objectives that matches that of the electorate. In the case of operational independence, the desideratum must surely be professional competence. There is no good reason to believe that this can best be ascertained by an appeal to a democratic election, whereas there is no better way than that of aligning preferences over value judgements between the ruled and their government. So, once a democratically elected government has decided on a central bank's objective, there is then no case for democratic election to the central bank itself. By the same token there would seem little, or no, case for seeking to make an MPC representative in its make-up of the community at large. Few would require that surgeons in a particular hospital should reflect the geographical, gender, ethnic, religious and sectoral split of the community more widely (though at the same time all should have a fair chance of entry into each profession, and none should be barred because of their personal background from establishing and using their professional skills). Moreover, the choice of someone as representative of some faction of the community might make that person feel that they had to alter their arguments, and their vote, on behalf of their own group; and that would tend to cause others to shift to an offsetting bias. This could, indeed, politicise what should be a technical decision. For that same reason the decision of the Governing Council of the European System of Central Banks *not* to reveal the individual arguments and positions of its members, especially the national central bank governors, is entirely appropriate.

If the touchstone for selection to work in an operationally independent MPC should be professional competence, then appointment would appear to be preferable to election by a non-professional electorate. That raises the question of how such an appointment should be made, and whether it should be subject to confirmation, for example by a select committee of Parliament, but that is a much wider and more general question, and one much more suited to a political scientist than to a monetary economist.

So far we have focused on institutional and constitutional issues. This is because in the long run such issues determine how well the overall system performs. In the short run a brilliant individual can make even a poorly designed institution work well; an example could be Benjamin Strong in the early years of the Federal Reserve Board in the USA. But what one wants is an institution sufficiently well designed to work with ordinary mortals.

Conclusion

An operationally independent, inflation-targeting central bank has been an excellent innovation in institutional design. The next step is for this constitutional advance to become embedded in the context of the modern democratic state, somewhat akin to the independent judiciary.

Of course, there are differences in detail between the precise design of independent central banks in different countries, and these differences, though second-order in comparison with the basic concept, are not without some importance. For example, transparency and accountability are of paramount importance. They both encourage good decision-making and entrench the independence of the central bank against attacks on its democratic legitimacy. The design of the Bank of England Act puts the MPC at the forefront of good practice in this respect. This new regime is a credit to its various progenitors. It is straightforward, transparent and accountable.

References

Blinder, A. (1998), *Central Banking in Theory and Practice*, MIT Press, Cambridge, Mass.

Friedman, M. (1962), 'Should there be an Independent Monetary Authority?', in L. B. Yeager (ed.), *In Search of a Monetary Constitution*, Harvard University Press, Boston, Mass.

Kydland, F. E., & Prescott, E. C. (1977), 'Rules rather than discretion: The inconsistency of optimal plans', *Journal of Political Economy* 85 (3), June.

ABOUT THE IEA

The Institute is a research and educational charity (No. CC 235 351), limited by guarantee. Its mission is to improve understanding of the fundamental institutions of a free society with particular reference to the role of markets in solving economic and social problems.

The IEA achieves its mission by:

- a high-quality publishing programme
- conferences, seminars, lectures and other events
- outreach to school and college students
- brokering media introductions and appearances

The IEA, which was established in 1955 by the late Sir Antony Fisher, is an educational charity, not a political organisation. It is independent of any political party or group and does not carry on activities intended to affect support for any political party or candidate in any election or referendum, or at any other time. It is financed by sales of publications, conference fees and voluntary donations.

In addition to its main series of publications the IEA also publishes a quarterly journal, *Economic Affairs*, and has two specialist programmes – Environment and Technology, and Education.

The IEA is aided in its work by a distinguished international Academic Advisory Council and an eminent panel of Honorary Fellows. Together with other academics, they review prospective IEA publications, their comments being passed on anonymously to authors. All IEA papers are therefore subject to the same rigorous independent refereeing process as used by leading academic journals.

IEA publications enjoy widespread classroom use and course adoptions in schools and universities. They are also sold throughout the world and often translated/reprinted.

Since 1974 the IEA has helped to create a world-wide network of 100 similar institutions in over 70 countries. They are all independent but share the IEA's mission.

Views expressed in the IEA's publications are those of the authors, not those of the Institute (which has no corporate view), its Managing Trustees, Academic Advisory Council members or senior staff.

Members of the Institute's Academic Advisory Council, Honorary Fellows, Trustees and Staff are listed on the following page.

The Institute gratefully acknowledges financial support for its publications programme and other work from a generous benefaction by the late Alec and Beryl Warren.

The Institute of Economic Affairs
2 Lord North Street, Westminster, London SW1P 3LB
Tel: 020 7799 8900
Fax: 020 7799 2137
Email: iea@iea.org.uk
Internet: iea.org.uk

THE WINCOTT MEMORIAL LECTURES

13 The Pleasures and Pains of Modern Capitalism
GEORGE J. STIGLER
1982 *Occasional Paper 64* Out of print

14 Myth and Reality in Anti-Trust
ARTHUR SHENFIELD
1983 *Occasional Paper 66* Out of print

15 Economic Policy as a Constitutional Problem
JAN TUMLIR
1984 *Occasional Paper 70* Out of print

16 Two Cheers for Self-Interest
Some Moral Prerequisites of a Market Economy
SAMUEL BRITTAN
1985 *Occasional Paper 73* Out of print

17 Liberalisation for Faster Economic Growth
Internal and External Measures Required
HERBERT GIERSCH
1986 *Occasional Paper 74* Out of print

18 Mr Hammond's Cherry Tree
The Morphology of Union Survival
BEN ROBERTS
1987 *Occasional Paper 76* Out of print

26 Back from the Brink
An Appeal to Fellow Europeans Over Monetary Union
PEDRO SCHWARTZ
1997 *Occasional Paper 101* Out of print

27 The Conservative Government's Economic Record
An End of Term Report
NICHOLAS CRAFTS
1998 *Occasional Paper 104* £5.00

28 Understanding the Process of Economic Change
DOUGLASS C. NORTH
1999 *Occasional Paper 106* £5.00

29 Privatisation, Competition and Regulation
STEPHEN C. LITTLECHILD
2000 *Occasional Paper 110* £5.00

30 Anti-Liberalism 2000
The Rise of New Millennium Collectivism
DAVID HENDERSON
2001 *Occasional Paper 115* £7.50

31 Post-Communist Transition: Some Lessons
LESZEK BALCEROWICZ
2002 *Occasional Paper 127* £7.50

Wincott-Sponsored Research Publications

Capital Controls: A 'Cure' Worse than the Problem?
FORREST CAPIE
2002 *Research Monograph 56*, £10.00

Other papers recently published by the IEA include:

WHO, What and Why?

Transnational Government, Legitimacy and the World Health Organization
Roger Scruton
Occasional Paper 113; ISBN 0 255 36487 3
£8.00

The World Turned Rightside Up

A New Trading Agenda for the Age of Globalisation
John C. Hulsman
Occasional Paper 114; ISBN 0 255 36495 4
£8.00

The Representation of Business in English Literature

Introduced and edited by Arthur Pollard
Readings 53; ISBN 0 255 36491 1
£12.00

Anti-Liberalism 2000

The Rise of New Millennium Collectivism
David Henderson
Occasional Paper 115; ISBN 0 255 36497 0
£7.50

Capitalism, Morality and Markets

Brian Griffiths, Robert A. Sirico, Norman Barry & Frank Field

Readings 54; ISBN 0 255 36496 2

£7.50

A Conversation with Harris and Seldon

Ralph Harris & Arthur Seldon

Occasional Paper 116; ISBN 0 255 36498 9

£7.50

Malaria and the DDT Story

Richard Tren & Roger Bate

Occasional Paper 117; ISBN 0 255 36499 7

£10.00

A Plea to Economists Who Favour Liberty: Assist the Everyman

Daniel B. Klein

Occasional Paper 118; ISBN 0 255 36501 2

£10.00

Waging the War of Ideas

John Blundell

Occasional Paper 119; ISBN 0 255 36500 4

£10.00

The Changing Fortunes of Economic Liberalism

Yesterday, Today and Tomorrow
David Henderson
Occasional Paper 105 (new edition); ISBN 0 255 36520 9
£12.50

The Global Education Industry

Lessons from Private Education in Developing Countries
James Tooley
Hobart Paper 141 (new edition); ISBN 0 255 36503 9
£12.50

Saving Our Streams

The Role of the Anglers' Conservation Association in
Protecting English and Welsh Rivers
Roger Bate
Research Monograph 53; ISBN 0 255 36494 6
£10.00

Better Off Out?

The Benefits or Costs of EU Membership
Brian Hindley & Martin Howe
Occasional Paper 99 (new edition); ISBN 0 255 36502 0
£10.00

Buckingham at 25

Freeing the Universities from State Control
Edited by James Tooley
Readings 55; ISBN 0 255 36512 8
£15.00

Lectures on Regulatory and Competition Policy

Irwin M. Stelzer
Occasional Paper 120; ISBN 0 255 36511 X
£12.50

Misguided Virtue

False Notions of Corporate Social Responsibility
David Henderson
Hobart Paper 142; ISBN 0 255 36510 1
£12.50

HIV and Aids in Schools

The Political Economy of Pressure Groups and Miseducation
Barrie Craven, Pauline Dixon, Gordon Stewart & James Tooley
Occasional Paper 121; ISBN 0 255 36522 5
£10.00

The Road to Serfdom

The Reader's Digest *condensed version*
Friedrich A. Hayek
Occasional Paper 122; ISBN 0 255 36530 6
£7.50

Bastiat's *The Law*

Introduction by Norman Barry
Occasional Paper 123; ISBN 0 255 36509 8
£7.50

A Globalist Manifesto for Public Policy

Charles Calomiris
Occasional Paper 124; ISBN 0 255 36525 X
£7.50

Euthanasia for Death Duties

Putting Inheritance Tax Out of Its Misery
Barry Bracewell-Milnes
Research Monograph 54; ISBN 0 255 36513 6
£10.00

Liberating the Land

The Case for Private Land-use Planning
Mark Pennington
Hobart Paper 143; ISBN 0 255 36508 X
£10.00

IEA Yearbook of Government Performance 2002/2003

Edited by Peter Warburton
Yearbook 1; ISBN 0 255 36532 2
£15.00

Britain's Relative Economic Performance, 1870–1999

Nicholas Crafts
Research Monograph 55; ISBN 0 255 36524 1
£10.00

Should We Have Faith in Central Banks?

Otmar Issing
Occasional Paper 125; ISBN 0 255 36528 4
£7.50

The Dilemma of Democracy

Arthur Seldon

Hobart Paper 136 (reissue); ISBN 0 255 36536 5

£10.00

Capital Controls: a 'Cure' Worse Than the Problem?

Forrest Capie

Research Monograph 56; ISBN 0 255 36506 3

£10.00

The Poverty of 'Development Economics'

Deepak Lal

Hobart Paper 144 (reissue); ISBN 0 255 36519 5

£15.00

Should Britain Join the Euro?

The Chancellor's Five Tests Examined

Patrick Minford

Occasional Paper 126; ISBN 0 255 36527 6

£7.50

Post-Communist Transition: Some Lessons

Leszek Balcerowicz

Occasional Paper 127; ISBN 0 255 36533 0

£7.50

A Tribute to Peter Bauer

John Blundell et al.

Occasional Paper 128; ISBN 0 255 36531 4

£10.00

Employment Tribunals

Their Growth and the Case for Radical Reform

J. R. Shackleton

Hobart Paper 145; ISBN 0 255 36515 2

£10.00

Fifty Economic Fallacies Exposed

Geoffrey E. Wood

Occasional Paper 129; ISBN 0 255 36518 7

£12.50

A Market in Airport Slots

Keith Boyfield (editor), David Starkie, Tom Bass & Barry Humphreys

Readings 56; ISBN 0 255 36505 5

£10.00

To order copies of currently available IEA papers, or to enquire about
availability, please contact:

Lavis Marketing
IEA orders
FREEPOST LON21280
Oxford OX3 7BR

Tel: 01865 767575
Fax: 01865 750079
Email: orders@lavismarketing.co.uk

The IEA also offers a subscription service to its publications. For a single
annual payment, currently £40.00 in the UK, you will receive every
title the IEA publishes across the course of a year, invitations to events,
and discounts on our extensive back catalogue. For more information,
please contact:

Subscriptions
The Institute of Economic Affairs
2 Lord North Street
London SW1P 3LB

Tel: 020 7799 8900
Fax: 020 7799 2137
Website: www.iea.org.uk